MACBETH

William Shakespeare

Edited by
CEDRIC WATTS

WORDSWORTH CLASSICS

In loving memory of
MICHAEL TRAYLER
the founder of Wordsworth Editions

17

Readers who are interested in other titles from
Wordsworth Editions are invited to visit our website at
www.wordsworth-editions.com

For our latest list and a full mail-order service contact
Bibliophile Books, 5 Thomas Road, London E14 7BN
Tel: +44 (0) 207 515 9222   Fax: +44 (0) 207 538 4115
e-mail: orders@bibliophilebooks.com

Macbeth was first published by Wordsworth Editions Limited
in 1992. An edition with new introduction and notes appeared in 2000.
This edition, with new text and fully-revised apparatus, appeared in 2005.

ISBN 978 1 85326 035 3

Typeset in Great Britain by Antony Gray
Printed and bound by Clays Ltd, St Ives plc

CONTENTS

GENERAL INTRODUCTION

In the new Wordsworth Classics' Shakespeare Series, the inaugural volumes, *Romeo and Juliet*, *The Merchant of Venice* and *Henry V*, have been followed by *The Taming of the Shrew*, *A Midsummer Night's Dream*, *Much Ado about Nothing*, *Julius Cæsar*, *Hamlet*, *Twelfth Night*, *Measure for Measure*, *Othello*, *Macbeth*, *King Lear*, *The Winter's Tale* and *The Tempest*. Previously, the Wordsworth Shakespeare volumes often adopted, by arrangement, an earlier Cambridge University Press text. The new series, however, consists of fresh editions specially commissioned for Wordsworth Classics. Each play in this emergent Shakespeare Series is accompanied by a standard apparatus, including an introduction, explanatory notes and a glossary. The textual editing takes account of recent scholarship, while giving the material a careful reappraisal. The apparatus is, however, concise rather than elaborate. We hope that the resultant volumes prove to be handy, reliable and helpful. Above all, we hope that, from Shakespeare's works, readers will derive pleasure, wisdom, provocations, challenges, and insights: insights into his culture and ours, and into the era of civilisation to which his writings have made (and continue to make) such potently influential contributions. Shakespeare's eloquence will, undoubtedly, re-echo 'in states unborn and accents yet unknown'.

CEDRIC WATTS
Series Editor

INTRODUCTION

Macbeth is one of Shakespeare's greatest tragedies: a darkly atmospheric drama of crime and punishment, of temptation, guilt, remorse and retribution. The portrayals of Macbeth himself and his wife display vividly the psychology of ambition, rationalised treachery and eventual disillusionment. Repeatedly the rich and often sinuously complex poetry gives general resonance to the particular situation, so that numerous speeches provide enduring epitomes of states of being which many of us, intermittently, may experience. Inner division, pangs of conscience, the pain of being ambushed by events, and desperate defiance: they are there; but so too is a vitality of expression and of enactment which offsets the play's sombre atmosphere

Macbeth is also a play which held political topicality for its earliest audiences. On the death of Queen Elizabeth in 1603, James VI, King of Scotland, became James I, King of England, thus uniting two realms. In the year of his accession, Shakespeare's company of players, the Chamberlain's Men, was formally taken into James's service and became the King's Men. The actors joined the honoured ranks in the procession to James's coronation in 1604, each player being supplied with over four metres of red cloth for the occasion; and William Shakespeare's name headed the list of recipients. James took a keen interest in drama, and Shakespeare's company appeared more frequently before him than they had before Elizabeth.[1]

Macbeth is believed to have been written between 1603 and 1606 (possibly during 1606), and the links between King James and this tragedy are evident. It is clearly no coincidence that soon after a Scottish monarch ascends the English throne, a Shakespearian drama about Scottish history appears. (The King preferred short plays, and *Macbeth* is among Shakespeare's shortest.) James had united two realms, so the play offers an anticipation of this: we see how Macbeth is overthrown by an alliance of Scots and Englishmen. Furthermore, the union is specifically prophesied to Macbeth in Act 4, Scene 1, as he responds in dismay to a vision of eight kings:

> What, will the line stretch out to th'crack of Doom?
> Another yet? A seventh? I'll see no more.
> And yet the eighth appears, who bears a glass
> Which shows me many more; and some I see
> That two-fold balls and treble sceptres carry.

The phrase 'two-fold balls' is usually taken to mean 'a pair of ceremonial orbs': James held one orb at his Scottish coronation and another at his English coronation. At the former ceremony he bore one sceptre and at the latter he bore two of them: hence, probably, the reference to 'treble sceptres'. The 'eighth' Stuart (or Stewart) king was James himself, boldly represented on stage, and flattered by the reference to his many successors. By the time of *Macbeth*, the Stuart kings of Scotland were: Robert II, Robert III, James I, James II, James III, James IV, James V and James VI. Mary, Queen of Scots, executed by Elizabeth, is tactfully excluded from the play's regal procession.[2] James claimed descent from Banquo (supposedly the progenitor of the Stuart line), so Banquo is depicted in the play as brave and conscientious. Even as he is assassinated, Banquo's concern is for the safety of his son Fleance – and thus for the potential royal dynasty. When King James visited Oxford in 1605, he was greeted by three 'fatal Sisters' who hailed him as the descendant of Banquo and the unifier of Britain. Banquo, however, was 'an imaginary figure invented by Hector Boece during the fifteenth century . . . to provide a proper ancestry for the Stewarts', and Macduff, too, seems to have been a chronicler's creation. William C. Carroll remarks:

> Hector Boece had first invented Banquo, Fleance, and the mythical genealogy of the Stuart descent – thus staking out a Stuart claim to the English throne via the Welsh monarch . . . [3]

In *Macbeth*, Shakespeare energetically aided the distortive process, the mythologising of history in order to strengthen a vulnerable dynasty.

Being a king entailed supernatural responsibilities. From time to time, victims of scrofula (a tuberculous disease of the lymphatic glands) were lined up after a religious service to be touched by James, because there was a traditional belief that direct contact with the monarch would effect a cure. In *Macbeth*, Act 4, Scene 3, we are reminded that this custom was established by Edward the Confessor, the virtuous King Edward who reigned from 1042 to 1066 and was proclaimed a saint in 1161. A doctor assures Malcolm that the procedure is effective: obviously, the King transmits God's therapeutic powers. 'To the succeeding royalty' (including James) 'he leaves / The healing benediction.' The disease was known as 'The Evil' or 'The King's Evil', and there survives an eye-witness account of the thaunmaturgic procedure as followed by James I.[4] After an Anglican service, and in the presence of a bishop and another clergyman,

> the Royal Physician brought a little girl, two boys, and a tall strapping youth, who were afflicted with incurable diseases ([known as] the Evil), and bade them kneel down before his Majesty; and as the Physician had already examined the disease (which he is always obliged to do, in order that no deception may be practised), he then pointed out the affected part in the neck of the first child to his Majesty, who thereupon touched it, pronouncing these words: *Le Roy vous touche, Dieu vous guery* (the King touches, may God heal thee!) and then hung a rose-noble [a gold coin] round the neck of the little girl with a white silk ribbon. He did the same with the other three . . .

Perhaps Shakespeare was unaware that James found the ceremony so 'very distasteful' that 'it is said he would willingly abolish it'. The custom was, however, intermittently maintained until the death of Queen Anne in 1714.

Another – deliberately contrasting – connection between *Macbeth* and the new monarch is made evident from the play's outset, in its depiction of the witches (or 'Weyward Sisters'). In 1584, Reginald Scot had published *The Discoverie of Witchcraft*, a detailed argument that women who were denounced as witches actually possessed no magical powers. If they had really possessed them, Scot shrewdly commented, they would have exploited them to gain the beauty, wealth and honour which they so conspicuously lacked.[5] Such scepticism infuriated King James, who wrote *Dæmonologie* (1597, re-issued in 1603), in which he maintained that witches really wielded hellish powers and should therefore be ruthlessly extirpated. James cited the Bible, which, in 1 Samuel 28, says that when Saul consulted the Witch of Endor, she summoned from the dead the spirit of Samuel.[6] Furthermore, according to Exodus 22:18, God had declared: 'Thou shalt not suffer a witch to live.' The completion of James's marriage to Princess Anne of Denmark and the return of the couple to Scotland (1589–90) had been repeatedly delayed by storms at sea; therefore, in Denmark and in Scotland, witches were blamed for the bad weather. The Earl of Bothwell was said to have conspired with such witches in the hope that James would drown. Naturally, the King took great interest in the ensuing trials, and personally interrogated some victims of torture. The reluctance of various women to confess until they were tortured 'witnesseth their guiltines[s]', the monarch sagely explained. He gave instructions that an accused person should be stripped and intimately inspected for the secret mark of Satan; and, if a bound woman floated on water instead of sinking, that, too, was obviously a sign of guilt. When a convicted female claimed to be pregnant, James commented to Chancellor Maitland: 'If ye find she be not, to the fire with her presently', and he added that she should also be publicly disembowelled.[7] In 1604, a year after James's accession, Parliament extended the range of punishments for activities associated with witchcraft. (A death-sentence for the main activity of invoking evil spirits had long been in place.) Subsequently, during the 17th century, many unfortunate women were denounced as witches, suffered torments and were judicially killed. Although in 1597 James had curbed investigations that he had initiated six years previously, in his *Basilikon Doron* (1599, re-issued in 1603,) the bisexual monarch advised his son that witchcraft, like wilful murder and sodomy, should be included among those 'horrible crimes that yee are bound in conscience never to forgive'.[8]

Henry VI, Part I, a play to which Shakespeare contributed, had portrayed Jeanne d'Arc, the patriotic French warrior, as a witch who offered her body and soul to devils. (Having been burnt at the stake in 1431, she would be declared a saint by the Pope in 1920.) A devil, or the Devil, answers the call of Margery Jourdain in *Henry VI, Part II*. Shakespeare's *Macbeth*, in turn, probably contributed to the climate of opinion in which superstitious cruelty occurred. Other dramatists were more circumspect. In the tragi-comedy *The Witch of Edmonton* (*circa* 1621, ascribed to Thomas Dekker and others), an old woman is persecuted by neighbours because she is 'poor, deformed, and ignorant'. She complains:

> Some call me witch,
> And being ignorant of myself, they go
> About to teach me how to be one . . . [9]

Since it is this persecution which drives her to sell her soul to the Devil, some sympathy is won for her. In contrast, the witches in *Macbeth* are irredeemably loathsome and malevolent. As James would have expected, they cause tempests which afflict voyagers, and they are associated with murder, treachery, and unnatural disturbances of many kinds.

Shakespeare's main source for *Macbeth* was a work by Raphael Holinshed and other writers, *The Chronicles of England, Scotland, and Ireland*: a mishmash of fact, legend and fiction. It first appeared in 1577, but Shakespeare evidently used the revised edition of 1587. The play is heavily indebted to it, both for large matters and for details. There are, however, some significant differences. The chronicler refers to the three strange women encountered by Macbeth as (according to the 'common opinion') 'the weird sisters, that is . . . the goddesses of destinie, or else some nymphs or feiries'; and, though in 'strange and wild apparell', they are far less repulsive than are the Weyward Sisters in the play. Another telling difference is that this source-work depicts the reign of Duncan as worse, and that of Macbeth as (for a while) better, than the play ever suggests. Though Duncan's reign was plagued by rebellions, the monarch himself was (according to the chronicler) partly to blame, because for years he ruled weakly and negligently. Certainly Macbeth, whose claims had some validity, gained the throne by killing Duncan, but various modern historians state that this death occurred during a battle; and the historic Duncan was younger than his counterpart in the play.[10] *The Chronicles* say that Macbeth proved eventually to be a bloodthirsty tyrant. Nevertheless, initially, and for a considerable time, his reign (1040–54) was strong and wise.

Makbeth . . . used great liberalitie towards the nobles of the realme, thereby to win their favour, and when he saw that no man went about to trouble him, he set his whole intention to mainteine justice, and to punish all enormities and abuses, which had chanced through the feeble and slouthfull administration of Duncane . . .

In the beginning of his reigne he accomplished manie woorthie acts, verie profitable to the commonwealth . . . [11]

He introduced 'manie holesome laws and statutes'; the people enjoyed 'the blissefull benefit of good peace and tranquillitie'; and he 'was accounted the sure defense and buckler of innocent people'.[12] Furthermore, according to Holinshed, Banquo was Macbeth's main accomplice in the murder of Duncan and the seizure of power:

At length therefore, communicating his purposed intent with his trustie friends, amongst whome Banquho was the chiefest, upon confidence of their promised aid, he [Macbeth] slue the king . . . Then having a companie about him of such as he had made privie to his enterprise, he caused himselfe to be proclaimed king . . . [13]

For the method used to dispatch Duncan, for the ruthless urgings by an ambitious wife, and for imagery associating the killing of a king with a disruption of nature, Shakespeare drew on Holinshed's account of the murder of a different monarch, King Duff, by Donwald, a castellan. This crime took place more than seventy years before Macbeth seized power in Scotland. Thus, history, legend and fantasy become deceptively blended.

Shakespeare was fully entitled to make free adaptations in the interests of theatrical cogency; but it is hard to escape the conclusion that the playwright was also prepared to adapt and alter the materials of the chronicle so as to flatter King James and to reinforce a traditional interlinkage of sound monarchy, divine favour, patriarchy and masculine control. In some obvious features, *Macbeth* celebrates superstition and aids intolerance. James had recognised that a belief in witchcraft, and particularly a belief in the objective reality of a devil who had a special interest in opposing the monarch, strengthened the principle of the divine right of kings, and demonstrated that James himself bore a particularly sacred aura. In any case, he maintained, 'Kings are called Gods by the propheticall

King David, because they sit upon GOD his Throne in the
earth . . . '[14]

  In *The Trew Law of Free Monarchies*, James argued that even a
wicked monarch should not be judged by his subjects, for God
alone could judge a king. (This is the 'divine right' principle.)
James wrote:

> The wickednesse thérefore of the King can never make them
> that are ordained to be judged by him, to become his Judges.[15]

Certainly, Shakespeare's play invites approval of a successful re-
bellion against a monarch; but it makes clear that King Macbeth is
to be regarded as an exceptional case. Macbeth is repeatedly
associated with supernatural evil and with 'unnatural' corruption,
while his enemies are systematically associated with supernatural
virtue and with the restoration of 'natural' order. (Much is made of
'The King's Touch', as we have noted, and Malcolm invokes God
when assuring Macduff that he is of unstained purity.) Macbeth has
been 'unnatural', a traitor to what should be regarded as morally
natural, in murdering Duncan, who is his monarch, his cousin, his
benefactor and his guest. Lady Macbeth has rebelled against natural
bonds in a diversity of ways. One is by denouncing 'the milk of
human kindness' in her husband; another is by taking command
when he hesitates to carry out the killing; and another is by
denying her womanly nature during, for instance, this witch–like
conjuration:

>   Come, you spirits
> That tend on mortal thoughts, unsex me here,
> And fill me, from the crown to the toe, top-full
> Of direst cruelty: make thick my blood,
> Stop up th'accéss and passage to remorse,
> That no compunctious visiting of nature
> Shake my fell purpose, nor keep peace between
> Th'effect and it. Come to my woman's breasts,
> And take my milk for gall, you murth'ring ministers,
> Wherever in your sightless substances
> You wait on nature's mischief. Come, thick night,
> And pall thee in the dunnest smoke of Hell...

  The crimes of Macbeth, abetted by his wife, are repeatedly

depicted by the play as breaches not only of conventional morality
but also of religious commandments and, indeed, of the very fabric
of nature. The witches are grossly unnatural in appearance, being
female but bearded; they relish blasphemy, infanticide and filth;
and they inflict storms and disruption. To them, indeed, 'Fair is
foul, and foul is fair' – words echoed ominously in Macbeth's 'So
foul and fair a day I have not seen'. On the night of the murder of
Duncan, chimneys are blown down, screams and lamentations are
heard in the air, and 'some say, the earth / Was feverous and did
shake'. Afterwards, the day is as dark as night, a falcon is killed by
an owl, and Duncan's horses devour each other.[16] Imagery of
darkness becomes potently pervasive, as in Macbeth's later words:

> Come, seeling night,
> Scarf up the tender eye of pitiful day,
> And with thy bloody and invisible hand
> Cancel and tear to pieces that great bond
> Which keeps me pale! Light thickens, and the crow
> Makes wing to th'rooky wood:
> Good things of day begin to droop and drowse,
> While night's black agents to their prey do rouse.

Such imagery of darkness, the eerie and the uncanny, and of
nature being disrupted and perverted, helps to make *Macbeth* one
of the most potently atmospheric of plays. With apt irony,
Macbeth's downfall is achieved by *benign* instances of the 'unnatural'. Macbeth cannot be defeated by a man 'of woman born';
but he can be defeated by Macduff, who was not 'born' but
rather 'untimely ripped' from his mother by Cæsarean section.
Macbeth cannot be overthrown until 'Birnam Forest come to
Dunsinane'; but that is what happens when his advancing foes use
foliage as camouflage.

  To readers who are sympathetically attuned to traditional Christi-
anity and to past eras' notions of a divinely-ordained co-ordination
of human values with the natural environment, *Macbeth* will seem a
thoroughly logical drama. To a sceptical reader (perhaps sceptical
about both Shakespeare's prestige and conventional religious teach-
ings), the play may instead seem to offer an elaborate mystification of
morality, 'mystification' here meaning a falsifying rhetorical linkage
of the moral with the supernatural. In addition, if that person has

republican sympathies, the association of good monarchy with divine favour will be a feature which strains the customary 'suspension of disbelief'.[17] But such a reader may still appreciate various aspects of the work. In its dark atmospheric intensity and the sense of an interlinked disruption of a human psyche and the wider environment, *Macbeth* anticipates features of the Gothic tradition and of later expressionist art. It may bring to mind, for example, Büchner's *Woyzeck*, Emily Brontë's *Wuthering Heights*, Conrad's *Heart of Darkness*, Welles's *Citizen Kane* and Reed's *The Third Man*: all linked by their portrayal of the charisma of corruption. Furthermore, the poetically-enriched psychology of the work repeatedly rings true: as a study of guilt, it offers a critical anticipation of the relatively prolix agonisings in Dostoyevsky's *Crime and Punishment*.

In the play's concluding speech, Malcolm refers to Macbeth and Lady Macbeth as 'this dead butcher and his fiend-like Queen'. If that were an adequate summing-up, the work would be a morality-play and not a tragedy. What makes it a tragedy is largely our sense of the larger-than-life qualities of the two main protagonists. The rendering of Lady Macbeth's passionate ambition and of her obsessive goading of her husband to the murder is powerfully eloquent. Then, however, her steely resolution begins to buckle. She remarks of Duncan: 'Had he not resembled / My father as he slept, I had done't'; and, when Macbeth returns to her after the deed, his hands bloodstained, his mind in anxious turmoil, she says: 'These deeds must not be thought / After these ways: so, it will make us mad.' His response: 'Methought I heard a voice cry "Sleep no more! / Macbeth doth murther sleep!" '. Later, he will 'lack the season of all natures, sleep'; and, more dramatically, she, her mind breaking under the strain of guilt, will sleep-walk in nightmare: 'Here's the smell of the blood still: all the perfumes of Arabia will not sweeten this little hand'. (So much for her claim that 'A little water clears us of this deed'.) Guilt and repression take their revenge, but one which reveals her ordinary vulnerable humanity as she declines to an early death, apparently suicide: she, 'as 'tis thought, by self and violent hands / Took off her life'.

As for Macbeth himself: his career and psychology are intensely and convincingly rendered. There's the early vacillation and uncertainty, his ambition grappling with scruples and hesitations until: 'We will proceed no further in this business.' Then there's his gradual responsiveness to his wife's goading, challenging, encouragement and deft connivance. 'I dare do all that may become a man', he says; and the distinction between true and false manliness becomes one of the keys of the thematic structure. (Compare Macduff's 'But I must also feel it as a man', in Act 4, Scene 3.)[18] Apparently hardened by the first murder, Macbeth is led on to further killings. As his wife had said: 'Nought's had, all's spent, / Where our desire is got without content'; so, after the death of Duncan, there follows the murder of Banquo, and then of Lady Macduff and her children, while Macbeth recognises the weary progress to which he is committed:

> I am in blood
> Stepped in so far that, should I wade no more,
> Returning were as tedious as go o'er . . .

Indeed, in his case, one of the most powerful humanising characteristics is his increasing recognition of the hollowness of his achievement as his way of life falls 'into the sere, the yellow leaf', without honour or friends; and his wife's eventual death prompts one of the finest speeches that Shakespeare ever wrote:

> She should have died hereafter:
> There would have been a time for such a word.
> Tomorrow, and tomorrow, and tomorrow,
> Creeps in this petty pace from day to day,
> To the last syllable of recorded time;
> And all our yesterdays have lighted fools
> The way to dusty death. Out, out, brief candle!
> Life's but a walking shadow, a poor player,
> That struts and frets his hour upon the stage,
> And then is heard no more. It is a tale
> Told by an idiot, full of sound and fury,
> Signifying nothing.

In its depressive tone and sense, it is utterly appropriate to the situation (his wife's death just before the fateful battle, coupled with his recognition that he has 'supped full with horrors'). Theologically, it marks his descent into the mortal sin of utter despair; indeed, it is blasphemous in its assertion that life is pointless and absurd. Of course, what gives the speech its general resonance is its ability to summarise, in such quotably forceful phrases, emotions and notions that most of us experience at one time or another, perhaps in times of bereavement, depression, weariness or tedium. It is culturally proleptic, anticipating bleakly-sceptical modern works: one thinks of Conrad's Decoud, who 'beheld the universe as a succession of incomprehensible images', of Sartre's Roquentin, discovering that 'Everything is gratuitous, that park, this town, and myself . . . superfluous', and of the fatalistic characters in Samuel Beckett's plays.[19]

In *Macbeth*, however, the speech's negativity is offset not only by the moral course of the plot, which does not 'signify nothing', but also by its own sensuous eloquence, in which the rhythms and the dense patternings of alliteration and assonance provide the pleasures of euphonious enrichment of linguistic textures. The persuasive quality is such that there is no disruption of the dramatic illusion when the actor who is speaking invokes the image of an inferior 'poor player' who struts and frets. One of the dramatic functions of this passage is to augment our sense of the paradoxical complexity of Macbeth, in whom the brutal consorts with the introspective, the disillusioned with the courageous. Though the witches foretell but cannot compel,[20] he has been misled by them and initially swayed by his wife's passionate arguments. Without such prompting, his murderous ambition might have remained dormant. Finally, even when he begins to feel 'aweary of the sun', he will still go down fighting: 'At least we'll die with harness on our back!'. Indeed, as his downfall becomes inevitable, he may elicit from us some of the sympathy that we accord to the courageous underdog or to the defiant villain who fights on against overwhelming odds. Blake and Shelley claimed that the true hero of Milton's *Paradise Lost* was not God but Satan – a characterisation probably influenced by that of Macbeth. Though Macbeth's turpitude is obvious, so also is his degree of humanity (evident in his early doubts and his later disillusionment), and so are the abilities to recognise tardily his doomed situation and to respond with grit and Stoicism.

He acknowledges his impulses with dread, submits to them half-knowing the consequences, and watches himself destroying himself in a long suicide of the soul.[21]

In any case, if we look closely at the opposition, we find that

Malcolm and Macduff make rather odd representatives of the cause
of virtue and order. When Malcolm tests Macduff in the archaically
ritualistic dialogue of Act 4, Scene 3, he lies outrageously, and
Macduff seems disgraceful in being prepared to condone so many
sins (including lechery, avarice and murder) before at last pro-
testing. When, in response, Malcolm then presents himself as a
paragon of virtue, he seems too good to be true. If we consider
Macduff 's character, we notice that he did indeed (to Malcolm's
bewilderment) abandon to their doom his wife and children; so
that, if Macbeth fatally over-valued the counsels of women (offered
by the witches and Lady Macbeth), Macduff here seems fatally to
under-value the love of one woman, the wife to whom he owes
loyalty. When, in the last scene, he proudly enters, bearing
Macbeth's head on a pole, the gory image casts an ironic shadow on
the claim that God and divine providence have prevailed. The play
had begun with reminders of the horrors of war: Macdonwald was
'unseamed . . . from the nave to th'chops' by Macbeth, who then
'fixed his head upon [the] battlements'; and it ends with further
reminders of such horrors and of the primitive ethos of martial
politics. One critic has even remarked:

> Macduff at the end stands in the same relation to Malcolm as
> Macbeth did to Duncan at the beginning. He is now the king-
> maker on whom the legitimate monarch depends, and the
> recurrence of the whole sequence may be anticipated . . . [22]

This quoted view represents not only an increasing critical
uneasiness about strongly conservative features in the play but also
a related desire to 'read against the grain' or to magnify those
details of the text which provide a basis for the questioning of
traditional orthodoxies. Just as Shakespeare freely adapted *The
Chronicles*, so directors of *Macbeth* may freely adapt Shakespeare.
At the end of Roman Polanski's film of *Macbeth*, Donalbain
approaches and enters the witches' lair – implying that he may
seek to overthrow Malcolm, as Macbeth had formerly sought to
supplant Duncan. In Penny Woolcock's *Macbeth on the Estate*,
Malcolm is assassinated by Fleance.[23] Thus Shakespeare's own
practice provides warrant for interpretations which may radically
transform the apparent ideological implications of the received
text.

Murky, violent, powerful and turbulent, *Macbeth* provides tempting material for protean development. Like the Wayward Sisters, it offers provocative but perilous promptings to the ambitious.

NOTES TO THE INTRODUCTION

1 F. E. Halliday: *A Shakespeare Companion 1564–1964* (Harmondsworth: Penguin, 1964), p. 93.

2 Shakespeare may have known the Stuart family tree as published in John Leslie's *De origine, moribus, et rebus gestis Scotorum*, 1578. This tree is reproduced in *Narrative and Dramatic Sources of Shakespeare*, ed. Geoffrey Bullough, Vol. VII (London: Routledge & Kegan Paul; New York: Columbia University Press, 1973), p. 517. An accurate magical glass could have shown the beheading of Charles I in 1649 after his defeat by Oliver Cromwell.

3 The formal address by the Sisters is reprinted in *Narrative and Dramatic Sources*, Vol. VII, pp. 470–72. They claim to be the very Sisters (or 'Fates') who had originally prophesied the success of Banquo's line. They repeat 'All hail!' and 'Hail!', as do their counterparts in the play. The same volume, pp. 433–4, says that Banquo, Fleance and Macduff were inventions by chroniclers. Muriel Bradbrook states that Boece invented Banquo: see her 'The Origins of *Macbeth*' in *Shakespeare: 'Macbeth': A Casebook*, ed. John Wain (Basingstoke: Macmillan, 1994), pp. 237 and 242–3. The Carroll quotation is from his ' "Two truths are told": Afterlives and Histories of Macbeths' in *Shakespeare Survey, 57: 'Macbeth' and Its Afterlife*, ed. Peter Holland (Cambridge: Cambridge University Press, 2004), pp. 69–80; quotation, p. 73.

4 W. B. Rye: *England as Seen by Foreigners* (London: Smith, 1865), p. 151.

5 Reginald Scot: *The Discoverie of Witchcraft* [1584] (rpt., with Introduction by Montague Summers: New York: Dover, 1972), pp. 4–5. Scot mocked *Malleus Maleficarum*, a Roman Catholic treatise defining modes of witchcraft and exorcism.

6 James insisted that the spirit of Samuel was impersonated by Satan. See his *Dæmonologie* [1597] (rpt., London: Bodley Head, 1924), pp. 3–5.

7 *Dæmonologie*, pp. 30 (reluctance to confess), 33 (secret mark) and 80 (secret mark and the water-test). Comment to Maitland: see *Letters of King James VI and I*, ed. G. P. V. Akrigg (University of California Press, 1984), p. 114.

8 *Basilikon Doron* in *The Political Works of James I Reprinted from the Edition of 1616*, ed. C. H. McIlwain (New York: Russell & Russell, 1965), p. 20. (In this and later quotations, I modernise a few spelling conventions; for instance, here I modernise 'neuer to forgiue' as 'never to forgive'.)

9 *The Witch of Edmonton* in *Thomas Dekker*, ed. Ernest Rhys (London: Fisher Unwin; New York: Scribner's Sons; n.d.), p. 408.

10 For instance, Gordon Donaldson's *Scottish Kings* (London: Batsford, 1967), p. 13, says that Duncan was 'killed in battle'. *The New Penguin History of Scotland* (London: Penguin, 2001), p. 78, however, suggests 'assassination'. The Holinshed group states that Macbeth 'slue the king at Enverns, or (as some say) at Botgosuane'. See: Raphael Holinshed and others: *The Chronicles of England, Scotland, and Ireland*, Vol. II [1587], extracted in *Narrative and Dramatic Sources*, Vol. VII, p. 496.

11 *Narrative and Dramatic Sources*, Vol. VII, pp. 497 and 505.

12 *Narrative and Dramatic Sources*, Vol. VII, pp. 498 and 497. In 2005, members of the Scottish Parliament expressed their regret that Macbeth was 'misportrayed in the inaccurate Shakespeare play when he was in fact a successful Scottish king'. (*The Times*, 3 February 2005, p. 5.)

13 *Narrative and Dramatic Sources*, Vol. VII, p. 496.

14 James I: *The Trew Law of Free Monarchies* in *The Political Works of James I*, ed. C. H. McIlwain (New York: Russell & Russell, 1965), p. 54.

15 *The Trew Law of Free Monarchies*, p. 66. (I substitute the modern 'j' where the text has the archaic 'i'.) Although James does concede that God may use rebellions to scourge wicked kings, he reiterates that true Christians should never join any such rebellions, for they are 'monstrous and unnatural' (p. 70).

16 According to *The Chronicles* (in *Narrative and Dramatic Sources*, Vol. VII, pp. 483–4), after the murder of King Duff by Donwald:

> For the space of six moneths togither . . . there appeered no sunne by day, nor moone by night in anie part of the realme, but still was the skie covered with continuall clouds, and sometimes suche outragious windes arose, with lightenings and tempests, that the people were in great feare of present destruction.
>
> Monstrous sights also that were seene within the Scotish kingdome that yeere were these, horsses in Louthian, being of singular beautie and swiftnesse, did eate their owne flesh, and would in no wise taste anie other meate . . . There was a spar-hawke also strangled by an owle.

17 '[T]hat willing suspension of disbelief for the moment, which constitutes poetic faith': Samuel Taylor Coleridge, *Biographia Literaria*, Vol. II (London: Fenner, 1817), p. 2.

18 In a commentary on the play, Emma Smith remarks: 'Manliness is sometimes synonymous with humanity, sometimes with extreme brutality, in a conflict of meanings which represent, in miniature, the complex value-systems of the warlike society of Macbeth's Scotland.' See William Shakespeare: *Five Great Tragedies* (Ware: Wordsworth Editions, 1998), p. 442.

19 Decoud: see Joseph Conrad: *Nostromo*, ed. Cedric Watts (London: Everyman Orion, 1995), p. 361. Roquentin: see Jean-Paul Sartre: *Nausea*, tr. Robert Baldick (Harmondsworth: Penguin, 1965), p. 188. Beckett: ubiquitously, but notably in *Waiting for Godot* (London: Faber & Faber, 1956), pp. 89–91. A reviewer of a 2005 production of Shakespeare's play said that Simon Russell Beale's Macbeth 'turns into a dry-voiced replica of Sam Beckett's *End Game*'. (Benedict Nightingale: 'Something evil this way comes . . . ': *The Times*, 21 January 2005, p. 20. This production was directed by John Caird.)

20 They foresee the outcome of Macbeth's free choices; but their deceptive prophecies influence those choices, as does Lady Macbeth's ambition.

21 Benedict Nightingale, *op. cit.*, p. 20.

22 Alan Sinfield: '*Macbeth*: History, Ideology and Intellectuals' in *New Casebooks: 'Macbeth': William Shakespeare*, ed. Alan Sinfield (Basingstoke: Macmillan, 1992), p. 128. *The Chronicles* tell us that although Malcolm was not overthrown, his reign was troubled by moral decadence, civil conflicts, and wars with two kings of England, William I and William II. Eventually, he was treacherously killed during a siege.

23. *Macbeth on the Estate*, a 1997 film for British television, is discussed in *Shakespeare Survey, 57*, pp. 45–53.

FURTHER READING
(in chronological order)

A. C. Bradley: *Shakespearean Tragedy*. London: Macmillan, 1904.

Shakespeare: 'Macbeth': A Casebook, ed. John Wain. London: Macmillan, 1968; revised edn., Basingstoke: Macmillan, 1994.

Narrative and Dramatic Sources of Shakespeare, Vol. VII, ed. Geoffrey Bullough. London: Routledge & Kegan Paul; New York: Columbia University Press; 1973.

Twentieth Century Interpretations of 'Macbeth': A Collection of Critical Essays, ed. Terence Hawkes. Englewood Cliffs, N.J.: Prentice-Hall, 1977.

The Woman's Part: Feminist Criticism of Shakespeare, ed. Carolyn Ruth Swift Lenz *et al.* Urbana, Ill.: University of Illinois Press, 1980.

Anthony Harris: *Night's Black Agents: Witchcraft and Magic in Seventeenth-Century English Drama*. Manchester: Manchester University Press, 1980.

John Bayley: *Shakespeare and Tragedy*. London: Routledge & Kegan Paul, 1981.

Focus on 'Macbeth', ed. John Russell Brown. London: Routledge & Kegan Paul, 1982.

Critical Essays on 'Macbeth', ed. Linda Cookson and Bryan Loughrey. Harlow: Longman, 1988.

'Macbeth': Critical Essays, ed. Samuel Schoenbaum. New York and London: Garland, 1991.

New Casebooks: 'Macbeth': William Shakespeare, ed. Alan Sinfield. Basingstoke: Macmillan, 1992.

Bernice W. Kliman: *Shakespeare in Performance: 'Macbeth'*. Manchester: Manchester University Press, 1992; 2nd edn., 2004.

M. M. Mahood: *Bit Parts in Shakespeare's Plays*. Cambridge: Cambridge University Press, 1992.

Gary Wills: *Witches and Jesuits: Shakespeare's 'Macbeth'*. New York and Oxford: New York Public Library and Oxford University Press, 1995.

Russ McDonald: *The Bedford Companion to Shakespeare*. Basingstoke: Macmillan, 1996.

Kenneth S. Rothwell: *A History of Shakespeare on Screen: A Century of Film and Television*. Cambridge: Cambridge University Press, 1999.

Nick Aitchison: *Macbeth: Man and Myth*. Stroud: Sutton Publishing, 1999.

Frank Kermode: *Shakespeare's Language*. London: Allen Lane, Penguin Press, 2000.

John Sutherland and Cedric Watts: *Henry V, War Criminal? and Other Shakespeare Puzzles*. Oxford: Oxford University Press, 2000.

A. F. Kinney: *Lies Like Truth: Shakespeare, Macbeth, and the Cultural Moment*. Detroit: Wayne State University Press, 2001.

Shakespeare: An Oxford Guide, ed. Stanley Wells and Lena Cowen Orlin. Oxford: Oxford University Press, 2003.

Shakespeare Survey, 57: 'Macbeth' and Its Afterlife, ed. Peter Holland. Cambridge: Cambridge University Press, 2004.

John Russell Brown: *Shakespeare Dancing: A Theatrical Study of the Plays*. Basingstoke: Palgrave Macmillan, 2005.

NOTE ON SHAKESPEARE

William Shakespeare was the son of a glover at Stratford-upon-Avon, and tradition gives his date of birth as 23 April, 1564; certainly, three days later, he was christened at the parish church. It is likely that he attended the local Grammar School but had no university education. Of his early career there is no record, though John Aubrey reports a claim that he was a rural schoolmaster. In 1582 Shakespeare married Anne Hathaway, with whom he had two daughters, Susanna and Judith, and a son, Hamnet, who died in 1596. How he became involved with the stage in London is uncertain, but by 1592 he was sufficiently established as a playwright to be criticised in print as a challengingly versatile 'upstart Crow'. He was a leading member of the Lord Chamberlain's company, which became the King's Men on the accession of James I in 1603. The players performed at a wide variety of locations: in the public theatre, at the royal court, in noblemen's houses, at colleges, and probably in the yards of inns. Being not only a playwright and an actor but also a 'sharer' (one of the owners of the company, entitled to a share of the profits), Shakespeare prospered greatly, as is proven by the numerous records of his financial transactions. Meanwhile, his sonnets expressed the poet's love for a beautiful young man and a 'dark lady'. Towards the end of his life, Shakespeare loosened his ties with London and retired to New Place, the large house in Stratford-upon-Avon which he had bought in 1597. He died on 23 April, 1616, and is buried in the place of his baptism, Holy Trinity Church. The earliest collected edition of his plays, the First Folio, was published in 1623, and its prefatory verse-tributes include Ben Jonson's famous declaration, 'He was not of an age, but for all time'.

ACKNOWLEDGEMENTS AND TEXTUAL MATTERS

In the present Wordsworth Classics' edition of *Macbeth*, I provide a newly-edited text which takes the First Folio as its basis. It supersedes the previous Wordsworth Classics' *Macbeth* (2000), which by arrangement used Dover Wilson's Cambridge text. I have consulted – and am indebted to – numerous editions of *Macbeth*, notably those by: H. H. Furness (the 'New Variorum': Philadelphia: Lippincott, 1874); John Dover Wilson (Cambridge: Cambridge University Press, 1947); Kenneth Muir ('The Arden Shakespeare' [1951]: London: Methuen, 1962; rpt., 1964); Peter Alexander ('The Tudor Shakespeare': London and Glasgow: Collins, 1951; rpt., 1966); G. Blakemore Evans *et al.* (*The Riverside Shakespeare*: Boston: Houghton Mifflin, 1974); Stanley Wells and Gary Taylor (*The Complete Works: Compact Edition*: Oxford: Oxford University Press, 1988); Nicholas Brooke ('The Oxford Shakespeare': Oxford: Oxford University Press, 1990; rpt., 1998); John F. Andrews ('The Everyman Shakespeare': London: Everyman Dent Orion, 1993); Stephen Greenblatt *et al.* (*The Norton Shakespeare*: New York and London: Norton, 1997); A. R. Braunmuller ('The New Cambridge Shakespeare': Cambridge: Cambridge University Press, 1997); and John Wilders ('Shakespeare in Production': Cambridge: Cambridge University Press, 2004). My Glossary adapts and revises Dover Wilson's.

As previously noted, *Macbeth* was written around 1603-6. A record survives of one performance at the Globe in 1610 or 1611, and it is highly probable that there were earlier performances. In 1623, *Macbeth* was formally registered, and the earliest extant text of the play is part of the First Folio, 1623; no previous quarto text is extant. A 'folio' is a book with relatively large pages, while a 'quarto' is a book with relatively small pages. More precisely, a folio volume is made of sheets of paper, each of which has been folded once to form two leaves and thus four pages, while each sheet of a quarto volume has been folded twice to form four leaves and thus eight pages. The First Folio (in recent times often designated 'F1') was the original 'collected edition' of Shakespeare's plays, published seven years after the playwright's death by two of the fellow-actors in his company, John Heminge (or Heminges) and Henry Condell.

The fact that there is no early quarto text of *Macbeth* may seem to make the editor's task easier, by eliminating the problem of deciding between quite different readings. (The variations between individual copies of F1 are few and small.) On the other hand, the editor's task is also harder, in the sense that there are no authoritative alternatives to consider if the copy-text seems faulty or obscure; and, in any case, posterity may thus lack some Shakespearian material that a quarto would have preserved. A Shakespearian play did not spring into existence fully-formed; it evolved. *Macbeth* is one of the shortest of his dramas, so it may have been subject to cuts. It seems to have been printed from a prompter's copy. The 'Heccat' scenes may have been initially furnished or (more likely) later added by Thomas Middleton, as two songs, 'Come away' and 'Black spirits', are indicated only by their openings in *Macbeth* but are given in full in Middleton's play *The Witch*. (In this Wordsworth edition, full texts of those songs are provided in the endnotes.)

The present edition of *Macbeth* offers a practical compromise between the F1 version, Shakespeare's intentions (insofar as they can be reasonably inferred) and modern requirements. I have followed F1's conventions somewhat more closely than have most editors. For instance, I have preserved (where they are logically and aurally satisfactory) many of its abundant colons and round brackets; and, in order to respect the sound-patterns, I have not changed F1's 'murther' and 'weyward' to 'murder' and 'weird'. I use a dash to indicate not only an interruption to a statement (or the start of a non-consecutive statement) but also a change of direction when a speaker turns from one addressee to another. The glossary explains archaisms and unfamiliar terms, while the annotations offer clarification of obscurities.

No edition of the play can claim to be definitive; but this one, which aims to combine fidelity, clarity and concise practicality, promises to be very useful.

THE TRAGEDY OF MACBETH

CHARACTERS

DUNCAN, *King of Scotland.*

MALCOLM, *Duncan's elder son.*

DONALBAIN, *Duncan's younger son.*

MACBETH, *Thane of Glamis, then of Cawdor; later, King of Scotland.*

LADY MACBETH; *later, Queen of Scotland.*

A medical DOCTOR *attending her.*

An ATTENDANT-GENTLEWOMAN.

BANQUO, *a Scottish thane, and* BANQUO'S GHOST.

FLEANCE, *Banquo's son.*

MACDUFF, *Thane of Fife.*

LADY MACDUFF.

SON *of the Macduffs.*

LENNOX, ROSS, ANGUS, CAITHNESS *and* MENTEITH, *Scottish thanes.*

SEYWARD, *Earl of Northumberland.*

YOUNG SEYWARD, *his son.*

An English DOCTOR.

SEVERAL MURDERERS.

SEYTON, *Macbeth's servant.*

HECCAT, *goddess of the witches.*

THREE WITCHES *(the Weyward Sisters) and* THREE OTHER WITCHES.

THREE APPARITIONS *and* VARIOUS SPIRITS.

An OLD MAN.

LORDS, THANES, ATTENDANTS, SERVANTS, *a* MESSENGER, *a* STEWARD *and* SOLDIERS *(including a* CAPTAIN, *a* DRUMMER *and* TRUMPETERS*).*

Locations: Scotland; England; Scotland again.

MACBETH[1]

ACT I, SCENE I.

Open ground. Thunder and lightning.

Enter THREE WITCHES.[2]

WITCH 1	When shall we three meet again?
	In thunder, lightning, or in rain?
WITCH 2	When the hurly-burly's done;
	When the battle's lost, and won.
WITCH 3	That will be ere the set of sun.
WITCH 1	Where the place?
WITCH 2	Upon the heath.
WITCH 3	There to meet with Macbeth.
WITCH 1	I come, Gray-Malkin.
WITCH 2	Padock calls.
WITCH 3	Anon![3]
ALL	Fair is foul, and foul is fair;
	Hover through the fog and filthy air.

10

[*Exeunt.*

SCENE 2.

A camp near Forres.

Alarum within. Enter KING DUNCAN, MALCOLM, DONALBAIN, LENNOX *and* ATTENDANTS, *meeting a bleeding* CAPTAIN.[4]

DUNCAN	What bloody man is that? He can report,
	As seemeth by his plight, of the revolt
	The newest state.
MALCOLM	This is the sergeant
	Who, like a good and hardy soldier, fought
	'Gainst my captivity. – Hail, brave friend!
	Say to the King the knowledge of the broil
	As thou didst leave it.
CAPTAIN	Doubtful it stood,
	As two spent swimmers that do cling together

And choke their art. The merciless Macdonwald   10
(Worthy to be a rebel, for to that
The multiplying villainies of nature
Do swarm upon him) from the Western Isles
Of kerns and gallowglasses is supplied,
And Fortune, on his damnèd quarrel smiling,
Showed like a rebel's whore; but all's too weak:
For brave Macbeth (well he deserves that name),
Disdaining Fortune, with his brandished steel,
Which smoked with bloody execution,
Like Valour's minion carved out his passage   20
Till he faced the slave;[5]
Which ne'er shook hands, nor bade farewell to him,
Till he unseamed him from the nave to th'chops,
And fixed his head upon our battlements.

DUNCAN   O valiant cousin! Worthy gentleman!

CAPTAIN   As whence the sun 'gins his reflection,
Shipwracking storms and direful thunders break;
So, from that spring whence comfort seemed to come,
Discomfort swells.[6] Mark, King of Scotland, mark!
No sooner justice had, with valour armed,   30
Compelled these skipping kerns to trust their heels,
But the Norweyan lord, surveying vantage,
With furbished arms and new supplies of men,
Began a fresh assault.

DUNCAN   Dismayed not this
Our captains, Macbeth and Banquo?

CAPTAIN   Yes;
As sparrows, eagles; or the hare, the lion.
If I say sooth, I must report they were
As cannons overcharged with double cracks,
So they doubly redoubled strokes upon the foe:
Except they meant to bathe in reeking wounds,   40
Or memorize another Gólgotha,
I cannot tell . . .
But I am faint; my gashes cry for help.

DUNCAN   So well thy words become thee as thy wounds:
They smack of honour both. – Go get him surgeons.
                    [*Exeunt captain and attendants.*

Enter ROSS *and* ANGUS.

      Who comes here?

MALCOLM   The worthy Thane of Ross.

LENNOX   What a haste looks through his eyes! So should he look
      That seems to speak things strange.

ROSS   God save the King!

DUNCAN   Whence cam'st thou, worthy Thane?

ROSS   From Fife, great King,
      Where the Norweyan banners flout the sky
      And fan our people cold.   50
      Norway himself, with numbers terrible,[7]
      Assisted by that most disloyal traitor,
      The Thane of Cawdor, began a dismal conflict,
      Till that Bellona's bridegroom, lapped in proof,
      Confronted him with self-comparisons,[8]
      Point against point rebellious, arm 'gainst arm,
      Curbing his lavish spirit; and, to conclude,
      The victory fell on us.

DUNCAN   Great happiness!

ROSS   That now   60
      Sweno, the Norways' King, craves composition;
      Nor would we deign him burial of his men
      Till he disbursèd, at Saint Colmè's Inch,[9]
      Ten thousand dollars to our general use.

DUNCAN   No more that Thane of Cawdor shall deceive
      Our bosom interest. Go pronounce his present death,
      And with his former title greet Macbeth.

ROSS   I'll see it done.

DUNCAN   What he hath lost, noble Macbeth hath won.

                                           [Exeunt.

SCENE 3.

A barren heath. Thunder.

Enter the THREE WITCHES.

WITCH I   Where hast thou been, sister?
WITCH 2   Killing swine.
WITCH 3   Sister, where thou?
WITCH I   A sailor's wife had chestnuts in her lap,
           And munched, and munched, and munched;
           'Give me', quoth I.
           'Aroynt thee, witch!', the rump-fed ronyon cries.
           Her husband's to Aleppo gone, master o'th' *Tiger*;
           But in a sieve I'll thither sail,
           And, like a rat without a tail,   10
           I'll do, I'll do, and I'll do.
WITCH 2   I'll give thee a wind.
WITCH I   Th'art kind.
WITCH 3   And I another.
WITCH I   I myself have all the other,
           And the very ports they blow,
           All the quarters that they know
           I'th'shipman's card.
           I'll drain him dry as hay;
           Sleep shall, neither night nor day,   20
           Hang upon his penthouse lid;
           He shall live a man forbid;
           Weary sev'nights nine times nine
           Shall he dwindle, peak, and pine;
           Though his bark cannot be lost,
           Yet it shall be tempest-tossed.[10]
           Look what I have.
WITCH 2   Show me, show me.
WITCH I   Here I have a pilot's thumb,
           Wracked as homeward he did come.   [*Drum within.* 30
WITCH 3   A drum, a drum:
           Macbeth doth come.

They dance in a ring.

ALL   The Weyward Sisters, hand in hand,
      Posters of the sea and land,
      Thus do go, about, about,
      Thrice to thine, and thrice to mine,
      And thrice again, to make up nine.
      Peace! The charm's wound up.

                                    [*They stop.*

Enter MACBETH *and* BANQUO.

MACBETH   So foul and fair a day I have not seen.
BANQUO   How far is't called to Forres? — What are these,   40
          So withered, and so wild in their attire,
          That look not like th'inhabitants o'th'earth,
          And yet are on't? — Live you? Or are you aught
          That man may question? You seem to understand me,
          By each at once her choppy finger laying
          Upon her skinny lips. You should be women,
          And yet your beards forbid me to interpret
          That you are so.[11]
MACBETH   Speak, if you can: what are you?
WITCH 1   All hail, Macbeth! Hail to thee, Thane of Glamis!
WITCH 2   All hail, Macbeth! Hail to thee, Thane of Cawdor!   50
WITCH 3   All hail, Macbeth! That shalt be King hereafter!
BANQUO   Good sir, why do you start, and seem to fear
          Things that do sound so fair? — I'th'name of truth,
          Are ye fantastical, or that indeed
          Which outwardly ye show? My noble partner
          You greet with present grace and great prediction
          Of noble having and of royal hope,
          That he seems rapt withal; to me you speak not.
          If you can look into the seeds of time
          And say which grain will grow and which will not,   60
          Speak then to me, who neither beg nor fear
          Your favours nor your hate.
WITCH 1   Hail!
WITCH 2   Hail!
WITCH 3   Hail!
WITCH 1   Lesser than Macbeth, and greater.

WITCH 2   Not so happy, yet much happier.

WITCH 3   Thou shalt get kings, though thou be none.
       – So all hail, Macbeth and Banquo!

WITCH 1   Banquo and Macbeth, all hail!   70

MACBETH   Stay, you imperfect speakers, tell me more.
       By Sinell's death,[12] I know I am Thane of Glamis,
       But how of Cawdor? The Thane of Cawdor lives,
       A prosperous gentleman; and to be King
       Stands not within the prospect of belief,
       No more than to be Cawdor. Say from whence
       You owe this strange intelligence, or why
       Upon this blasted heath you stop our way
       With such prophetic greeting. Speak, I charge you.
                        [*The witches vanish.*[13]

BANQUO   The earth hath bubbles, as the water has,   80
       And these are of them. Whither are they vanished?

MACBETH   Into the air; and what seemed corporal melted
       As breath into the wind. Would they had stayed!

BANQUO   Were such things here as we do speak about?
       Or have we eaten on the insane root
       That takes the reason prisoner?[14]

MACBETH   Your children shall be kings.

BANQUO   You shall be King.

MACBETH   And Thane of Cawdor too: went it not so?

BANQUO   To th'selfsame tune and words. – Who's here?

Enter ROSS *and* ANGUS.

ROSS   The King hath happily received, Macbeth,   90
       The news of thy success; and when he reads
       Thy personal venture in the rebels' fight,
       His wonders and his praises do contend
       Which should be thine or his. Silenced with that,
       In viewing o'er the rest o'th'self-same day,
       He finds thee in the stout Norweyan ranks,
       Nothing afeard of what thyself didst make
       Strange images of death. As thick as hail
       Came post with post,[15] and every one did bear
       Thy praises in his kingdom's great defence,   100
       And poured them down before him.

ANGUS   We are sent

To give thee from our royal master thanks;
Only to herald thee into his sight,
Not pay thee.

ROSS And for an earnest of a greater honour,
He bade me, from him, call thee Thane of Cawdor:
In which addition, hail, most worthy thane,
For it is thine.

BANQUO [*aside:*]   What, can the Devil speak true?

MACBETH The Thane of Cawdor lives: why do you dress me
In borrowed robes?

ANGUS   Who was the Thane lives yet,   110
But under heavy judgement bears that life
Which he deserves to lose. Whether he was combined
With those of Norway, or did line the rebel
With hidden help and vantage, or that with both
He laboured in his country's wrack, I know not;[16]
But treasons capital, confessed and proved,
Have overthrown him.

MACBETH [*aside:*]   Glamis, and Thane of Cawdor:
The greatest is behind. [*Aloud:*] Thanks for your pains.
[*Aside to Banquo:*] Do you not hope your children shall
                                        be kings,
When those that gave the Thane of Cawdor to me   120
Promised no less to them?

BANQUO [*aside to Macbeth:*]   That, trusted home,
Might yet enkindle you unto the crown,
Besides the Thane of Cawdor.[17] But 'tis strange;
And oftentimes, to win us to our harm,
The instruments of darkness tell us truths,
Win us with honest trifles, to betray's
In deepest consequence.
– Cousins, a word, I pray you.
                    [*He talks privately with Ross and Angus.*]

MACBETH [*aside:*]   Two truths are told,
As happy prologues to the swelling act
Of the imperial theme. [*Aloud:*] I thank you, gentlemen.   130
[*Aside:*] This supernatural soliciting
Cannot be ill; cannot be good. If ill,
Why hath it given me earnest of success,

Commencing in a truth? I am Thane of Cawdor.
If good, why do I yield to that suggestion
Whose horrid image doth unfix my hair
And make my seated heart knock at my ribs,
Against the use of nature? Present fears
Are less than horrible imaginings:
My thought, whose murther yet is but fantastical,[18]   140
Shakes so my single state of man that function
Is smothered in surmise, and nothing is
But what is not.

BANQUO [*to Ross and Angus:*] Look how our partner's rapt.

MACBETH [*aside:*] If chance will have me King, why, chance
                                        may crown me,
Without my stir.

BANQUO [*to Ross and Angus:*] New honours come upon him,
Like our strange garments, cleave not to their mould
But with the aid of use.

MACBETH [*aside:*]   Come what come may,
Time and the hour runs through the roughest day.[19]

BANQUO Worthy Macbeth, we stay upon your leisure.

MACBETH Give me your favour: my dull brain was wrought   150
With things forgotten. Kind gentlemen, your pains
Are registered where every day I turn
The leaf to read them.[20] Let us toward the King.
[*Aside to Banquo:*] Think upon what hath chanced; and
                                        at more time,
The interim having weighed it, let us speak
Our free hearts each to other.

BANQUO   Very gladly,

MACBETH Till then, enough. – Come, friends.

                                        [*Exeunt.*

SCENE 4.

Forres. A room in the palace.

Flourish. Enter DUNCAN, MALCOLM,
DONALBAIN, LENNOX *and* ATTENDANTS.

DUNCAN   Is execution done on Cawdor? Are not
Those in commission yet returned?

MALCOLM   My liege,
They are not yet come back. But I have spoke
With one that saw him die, who did report
That very frankly he confessed his treasons,
Implored your Highness' pardon, and set forth
A deep repentance: nothing in his life
Became him like the leaving it. He died
As one that had been studied in his death,
To throw away the dearest thing he owed   10
As 'twere a careless trifle.

DUNCAN   There's no art
To find the mind's construction in the face:
He was a gentleman on whom I built
An absolute trust.

Enter MALCOLM, BANQUO, ROSS *and* ANGUS.

[*To Macbeth:*]   O worthiest cousin,
The sin of my ingratitude even now
Was heavy on me. Thou art so far before,
That swiftest wing of recompense is slow
To overtake thee. Would thou hadst less deserved,
That the proportion both of thanks and payment
Might have been mine! Only I have left to say,   20
More is thy due than more than all can pay.

MACBETH   The service and the loyalty I owe,
In doing it, pays itself. Your Highness' part
Is to receive our duties; and our duties
Are, to your throne and state, children and servants,
Which do but what they should, by doing everything
Safe toward your love and honour.[21]

DUNCAN   Welcome hither:
I have begun to plant thee, and will labour
To make thee full of growing. – Noble Banquo,
That hast no less deserved, nor must be known   30
No less to have done so: let me enfold thee,
And hold thee to my heart.   [*He hugs Banquo.*

BANQUO   There if I grow,
The harvest is your own.

DUNCAN   My plenteous joys,
Wanton in fulness, seek to hide themselves
In drops of sorrow.[22] – Sons, kinsmen, thanes,
And you whose places are the nearest, know,
We will establish our estate upon
Our eldest, Malcolm, whom we name hereafter
'The Prince of Cumberland': which honour must
Not unaccompanied invest him only,   40
But signs of nobleness, like stars, shall shine
On all deservers. [*To Macbeth:*] From hence to Inverness,
And bind us further to you.

MACBETH The rest is labour, which is not used for you:
I'll be myself the harbinger, and make joyful
The hearing of my wife with your approach;
So humbly take my leave.

DUNCAN   My worthy Cawdor!

MACBETH [*aside:*] The Prince of Cumberland: that is a step
On which I must fall down, or else o'er-leap,
For in my way it lies. Stars, hide your fires;   50
Let not light see my black and deep desires:
The eye wink at the hand; yet let that be,
Which the eye fears, when it is done, to see.   [*Exit.*

DUNCAN True, worthy Banquo: he is full so valiant,
And in his commendations I am fed:
It is a banquet to me. Let's after him,
Whose care is gone before to bid us welcome.
It is a peerless kinsman.   [*Flourish. Exeunt.*

SCENE 5.

Inverness. Inisde Macbeth's castle.

Enter LADY MACBETH, *holding a letter.*

LADY M.   [*reads:*] 'They met me in the day of success; and I have
learned, by the perfect'st report, they have more in them
than mortal knowledge. When I burned in desire to
question them further, they made themselves air, into
which they vanished. Whiles I stood rapt in the wonder
of it, came missives from the King, who all-hailed me
'Thane of Cawdor', by which title, before, these Weyward
Sisters saluted me, and referred me to the coming-on of
time, with 'Hail, King that shalt be!'. This have I
thought good to deliver thee (my dearest partner of 10
greatness), that thou mightst not lose the dues of rejoicing
by being ignorant of what greatness is promised thee.
Lay it to thy heart, and farewell.'
Glamis thou art, and Cawdor, and shalt be
What thou art promised. Yet do I fear thy nature:
It is too full o'th'milk of human kindness
To catch the nearest way. Thou wouldst be great;
Art not without ambition, but without
The illness should attend it. What thou wouldst highly,
That wouldst thou holily; wouldst not play false,   20
And yet wouldst wrongly win. Thou'dst have,
                         great Glamis,
That which cries 'Thus thou must do', if thou have it,
And that which rather thou dost fear to do
Than wishest should be undone.[23] Hie thee hither,
That I may pour my spirits in thine ear
And chastise with the valour of my tongue
All that impedes thee from the golden round
Which Fate and metaphysical aid doth seem
To have thee crowned withal.

Enter a MESSENGER.

                      What is your tidings?

MESSENGER The King comes here tonight.

LADY M.   Thou'rt mad to say it!   30
          Is not thy master with him, who, were't so,
          Would have informed for preparation?

MESSENGER So please you, it is true: our Thane is coming:
          One of my fellows had the speed of him,
          Who, almost dead for breath, had scarcely more
          Than would make up his message.

LADY M.   Give him tending;
          He brings great news.   [*Exit messenger.*
                         The raven himself is hoarse
          That croaks the fatal entrance of Duncan
          Under my battlements.[24] Come, you spirits
          That tend on mortal thoughts, unsex me here,   40
          And fill me, from the crown to the toe, top-full
          Of direst cruelty: make thick my blood,
          Stop up th'accéss and passage to remorse,
          That no compunctious visitings of nature
          Shake my fell purpose, nor keep peace between
          Th'effect and it. Come to my woman's breasts,
          And take my milk for gall, you murth'ring ministers,
          Wherever in your sightless substances
          You wait on nature's mischief.[25] Come, thick night,
          And pall thee in the dunnest smoke of Hell,   50
          That my keen knife see not the wound it makes,
          Nor Heaven peep through the blanket of the dark
          To cry 'Hold, hold'!

                         Enter MACBETH.

                         Great Glamis! Worthy Cawdor!
          Greater than both, by the all-hail hereafter!
          Thy letters have transported me beyond
          This ignorant present, and I feel now
          The future in the instant.

MACBETH   My dearest love,
          Duncan comes here tonight.

LADY M.   And when goes hence?

MACBETH Tomorrow, as he purposes.

LADY M.   O, never
          Shall sun that morrow see!   60

Your face, my Thane, is as a book where men
May read strange matters. To beguile the time,
Look like the time: bear welcome in your eye,
Your hand, your tongue: look like th'innocent flower,
But be the serpent under't. He that's coming
Must be provided for; and you shall put
This night's great business into my dispatch,
Which shall to all our nights and days to come
Give solely sovereign sway and masterdom.

MACBETH We will speak further.

LADY M.   Only look up clear: 70
To alter favour, ever is to fear.[26]
Leave all the rest to me.   [*Exeunt.*

SCENE 6.

Evening. Outside the main gateway of Macbeth's castle.

Enter DUNCAN, MALCOLM, DONALBAIN, BANQUO, LENNOX,
MACDUFF, ROSS, ANGUS *and* ATTENDANTS.

DUNCAN This castle hath a pleasant seat; the air
Nimbly and sweetly recommends itself
Unto our gentle senses.

BANQUO   This guest of summer,
The temple-haunting martlet, does approve,
By his loved mansionry, that the heavens' breath
Smells wooingly here: no jutty, frieze,
Buttress, nor coign of vantage, but this bird
Hath made his pendant bed and procreant cradle:[27]
Where they must breed and haunt, I have observed
The air is delicate.

Enter LADY MACBETH.

DUNCAN   See, see: our honoured hostess!   10
The love that follows us sometime is our trouble,
Which still we thank as love. Herein I teach you
How you shall bid God 'ield us for your pains,
And thank us for your trouble.

LADY M.   All our service,[28]
          In every point twice done, and then done double,
          Were poor and single business to contend
          Against those honours, deep and broad, wherewith
          Your Majesty loads our house; for those of old,
          And the late dignities heaped up to them,
          We rest your hermits.

DUNCAN   Where's the Thane of Cawdor? 20
          We coursed him at the heels, and had a purpose
          To be his purveyor; but he rides well,
          And his great love (sharp as his spur) hath holp him
          To his home before us. Fair and noble hostess,
          We are your guest tonight.

LADY M.   Your servants ever
          Have theirs, themselves, and what is theirs, in compt,
          To make their audit at your Highness' pleasure,
          Still to return your own.

DUNCAN   Give me your hand:
          Conduct me to mine host. We love him highly,
          And shall continue our graces towards him.   30
          By your leave, hostess.   [Exeunt into the castle.

SCENE 7.

Night. Inside Macbeth's castle. Music of hautboys can be heard.

ATTENDANTS *enter, fix burning torches in place, and exeunt.*
A STEWARD *enters. He directs various* SERVANTS, *who cross the area,*
bearing the service and dishes for a banquet. Exeunt servants and steward.

Enter MACBETH *from the banqueting-chamber.*

MACBETH   If it were done, when 'tis done, then 'twere well
          It were done quickly: if th'assassination
          Could trammel up the consequence, and catch,
          With his surcease, success; that but this blow
          Might be the be-all and the end-all: here,
          But here, upon this bank and shoal of time,
          We'd jump the life to come.[29] But, in these cases,
          We still have judgement here, that we but teach

Bloody instructions, which, being taught, return
To plague th'inventor. This even-handed justice   10
Commends th'ingredience of our poisoned chalice
To our own lips. He's here in double trust:
First, as I am his kinsman and his subject,
Strong both against the deed; then, as his host,
Who should against his murtherer shut the door,
Not bear the knife myself. Besides, this Duncan
Hath borne his faculties so meek, hath been
So clear in his great office, that his virtues
Will plead like angels, trumpet-tongued, against
The deep damnation of his taking-off;   20
And pity, like a naked new-born babe,
Striding the blast, or Heaven's cherubin, horsed
Upon the sightless couriers of the air,[30]
Shall blow the horrid deed in every eye,
That tears shall drown the wind. I have no spur
To prick the sides of my intent, but only
Vaulting ambition, which o'erleaps itself,
And falls on th'other –

Enter LADY MACBETH.

                    How now, what news?

LADY M.   He has almost supped: why have you left the chamber?
MACBETH   Hath he asked for me?
LADY M.   Know you not he has?   30
MACBETH   We will proceed no further in this business.
He hath honoured me of late, and I have bought
Golden opinions from all sorts of people,
Which would be worn now in their newest gloss,
Not cast aside so soon.
LADY M.   Was the hope drunk
Wherein you dressed yourself? Hath it slept since?
And wakes it now, to look so green and pale
At what it did so freely? From this time,
Such I account thy love. Art thou afeard
To be the same in thine own act and valour   40
As thou art in desire? Wouldst thou have that
Which thou esteem'st the ornament of life,
And live a coward in thine own esteem,

Letting 'I dare not' wait upon 'I would',
Like the poor cat i'th'adage?[31]

MACBETH   Prithee, peace:
I dare do all that may become a man;
Who dares do more, is none.[32]

LADY M.   What beast was't then
That made you break this enterprise to me?
When you durst do it, then you were a man;
And, to be more than what you were, you would   50
Be so much more the man. Nor time nor place
Did then adhere, and yet you would make both;
They have made themselves, and that their fitness now
Does unmake you. I have given suck, and know
How tender 'tis to love the babe that milks me:
I would, while it was smiling in my face,
Have plucked my nipple from his boneless gums,
And dashed the brains out, had I so sworn as you
Have done to this.[33]

MACBETH   If we should fail?
LADY M.   We fail?
But screw your courage to the sticking place,[34]   60
And we'll not fail. When Duncan is asleep
(Whereto the rather shall his day's hard journey
Soundly invite him), his two chamberlains
Will I with wine and wassail so convince,
That memory, the warder of the brain,
Shall be a fume, and the receipt of reason
A limbec only. When in swinish sleep
Their drenchèd natures lie as in a death,
What cannot you and I perform upon
Th'unguarded Duncan? What not put upon   70
His spongy officers, who shall bear the guilt
Of our great quell?

MACBETH   Bring forth men-children only,
For thy undaunted mettle should compose
Nothing but males. Will it not be received,
When we have marked with blood those sleepy two
Of his own chamber, and used their very daggers,
That they have done't?

LADY M.   Who dares receive it other,
As we shall make our griefs and clamour roar
Upon his death?
MACBETH   I am settled, and bend up
Each corporal agent to this terrible feat.   80
Away, and mock the time with fairest show:
False face must hide what the false heart doth know.
                                        [*Exeunt.*

ACT 2, SCENE 1.

The courtyard of Macbeth's castle.

Enter FLEANCE *(holding a burning torch) and* BANQUO.[35]

BANQUO   How goes the night, boy?
FLEANCE   The moon is down; I have not heard the clock.
BANQUO   And she goes down at twelve.
FLEANCE   I take't, 'tis later, sir.
BANQUO   Hold, take my sword. There's husbandry in heaven:
          Their candles are all out. Take thee that too.
          A heavy summons lies like lead upon me,
          And yet I would not sleep. – Merciful powers,
          Restrain in me the cursèd thoughts that nature
          Gives way to in repose.   10

Enter a SERVANT *(holding a burning torch) and* MACBETH.

          [*To Fleance:*] Give me my sword.
          [*To the entrants:*]   Who's there?
MACBETH   A friend.
BANQUO   What, sir, not yet at rest? The King's a-bed.
          He hath been in unusual pleasure, and
          Sent forth great largess to your offices.
          This diamond he greets your wife withal,
          By the name of 'most kind hostess'; and shut up
          In measureless content.
MACBETH   Being unprepared,
          Our will became the servant to defect,
          Which else should free have wrought.[36]
BANQUO   All's well.   20
          I dreamt last night of the three Weyward Sisters:
          To you they have showed some truth.
MACBETH   I think not of them;
          Yet, when we can entreat an hour to serve,
          We would spend it in some words upon that business,
          If you would grant the time.
BANQUO   At your kind'st leisure.
MACBETH   If you shall cleave to my consent, when 'tis,

It shall make honour for you.

BANQUO   So I lose none
In seeking to augment it, but still keep
My bosom franchised and allegiance clear,
I shall be counselled.

MACBETH   Good repose the while.   30

BANQUO   Thanks, sir; the like to you.

                                    [*Exeunt Banquo and Fleance.*

MACBETH   – Go bid thy mistress, when my drink is ready,
She strike upon the bell. Get thee to bed. [*Exit servant.*
– Is this a dagger which I see before me,
The handle toward my hand? Come, let me
                                        clutch thee:
I have thee not, and yet I see thee still.
Art thou not, fatal vision, sensible
To feeling, as to sight? Or art thou but
A dagger of the mind, a false creation,
Proceeding from the heat-oppressèd brain?   40
I see thee yet, in form as palpable
As this which now I draw.   [*He draws his dagger.*
Thou marshall'st me the way that I was going,
And such an instrument I was to use.
Mine eyes are made the fools o'th'other senses,
Or else worth all the rest:[37] I see thee still,
And, on thy blade and dudgeon, gouts of blood,
Which was not so before. There's no such thing:
It is the bloody business which informs
Thus to mine eyes. Now, o'er the one half-world,   50
Nature seems dead, and wicked dreams abuse
The curtained sleep; witchcraft celebrates
Pale Heccat's offerings; and withered Murther,
Alarumed by his sentinel, the wolf,
Whose howl's his watch, thus with his stealthy pace,
With Tarquin's ravishing strides, towards his design
Moves like a ghost. Thou sure and firm-set earth,[38]
Hear not my steps, which way they walk, for fear
Thy very stones prate of my whereabout,
And take the present horror from the time,[39]   60
Which now suits with it. Whiles I threat, he lives:

Words to the heat of deeds too cold breath gives.

[*A bell rings.*

I go, and it is done: the bell invites me.
Hear it not, Duncan, for it is a knell
That summons thee to Heaven, or to Hell.

[*Exit.*

SCENE 2.

The same location.

Enter LADY MACBETH.

LADY M.   That which hath made them drunk hath made me bold;
What hath quenched them hath given me fire. —
                              Hark! — Peace:
It was the owl that shrieked, the fatal bellman,
Which gives the stern'st good–night.[40] He is about it:
The doors are open; and the surfeited grooms
Do mock their charge with snores. I have drugged
                              their possets,
That death and nature do contend about them,
Whether they live or die.

MACBETH   [*within:*]   Who's there? What ho!
LADY M.   Alack, I am afraid they have awaked,
And 'tis not done: th'attempt, and not the deed,   10
Confounds us. Hark! I laid their daggers ready;
He could not miss 'em. Had he not resembled
My father as he slept, I had done't.

                    Enter MACBETH, *holding two daggers
                    in his blood-stained hands.*

                              My husband!

MACBETH   I have done the deed. Didst thou not hear a noise?
LADY M.   I heard the owl scream, and the crickets cry.
Did not you speak?
MACBETH   When?
LADY M.   Now.
MACBETH   As I descended?

LADY M.	Ay.
MACBETH	Hark!
	Who lies i'th'second chamber?
LADY M.	Donalbain.
MACBETH	This is a sorry sight. 20
LADY M.	A foolish thought, to say 'a sorry sight'.
MACBETH	There's one did laugh in's sleep, and one cried 'Murther!',
	That they did wake each other: I stood and heard them;
	But they did say their prayers, and addressed them
	Again to sleep.
LADY M.	There are two lodged together.
MACBETH	One cried 'God bless us!', and 'Amen' the other,
	As they had seen me with these hangman's hands.[41]
	List'ning their fear, I could not say 'Amen',
	When they did say 'God bless us'.
LADY M.	Consider it not so deeply. 30
MACBETH	But wherefore could not I pronounce 'Amen'?
	I had most need of blessing, and 'Amen'
	Stuck in my throat.
LADY M.	These deeds must not be thought
	After these ways: so, it will make us mad.
MACBETH	Methought I heard a voice cry 'Sleep no more!
	Macbeth does murther sleep!': the innocent sleep,
	Sleep that knits up the ravelled sleeve of care,
	The death of each day's life, sore labour's bath,
	Balm of hurt minds, great Nature's second course,[42]
	Chief nourisher in life's feast, —
LADY M.	What do you mean? 40
MACBETH	Still it cried 'Sleep no more!' to all the house;
	'Glamis hath murthered sleep, and therefore Cawdor
	Shall sleep no more: Macbeth shall sleep no more!'
LADY M.	Who was it that thus cried? Why, worthy Thane,
	You do unbend your noble strength, to think
	So brainsickly of things. Go get some water,
	And wash this filthy witness from your hand.
	Why did you bring these daggers from the place?
	They must lie there: go carry them, and smear
	The sleepy grooms with blood.
MACBETH	I'll go no more: 50

I am afraid to think what I have done;
Look on't again I dare not.

LADY M.   Infirm of purpose!
Give me the daggers: the sleeping and the dead
Are but as pictures: 'tis the eye of childhood
That fears a painted Devil. If he do bleed,
I'll gild the faces of the grooms withal,
For it must seem their guilt.[43]   [*Exit. A knocking heard.*

MACBETH   Whence is that knocking?
How is't with me, when every noise appals me?
What hands are here? Ha! They pluck out mine eyes!
Will all great Neptune's ocean wash this blood   60
Clean from my hand? No; this my hand will rather
The multitudinous seas incarnadine,
Making the green one red.[44]

                         Enter LADY MACBETH.

LADY M.   My hands are of your colour; but I shame
To wear a heart so white.   [*Knocking.*
                         I hear a knocking
At the south entry; retire we to our chamber.
A little water clears us of this deed:
How easy is it then! Your constancy
Hath left you unattended.[45]   [*Knocking.*
                         Hark! More knocking.
Get on your night-gown, lest occasion call us   70
And show us to be watchers: be not lost
So poorly in your thoughts.
MACBETH   To know my deed, 'twere best not know myself.[46] –
                                                       [*Knocking.*
Wake Duncan with thy knocking! I would thou couldst!
                                                       [*Exeunt.*

SCENE 3.

Inside the southern gateway of the castle.
Intermittent knocking continues.

Enter the PORTER, *inebriated.*

PORTER   Here's a knocking indeed! If a man were porter of Hell
Gate, he should have old turning the key. [*Knocking.*
Knock, knock, knock! Who's there, i'th'name of Belze-
bub? Here's a farmer, that hanged himself on th'ex-
pectation of plenty: come in time; have napkins enow
about you: here you'll sweat for't.   [*Knocking.*
Knock, knock! Who's there, in th'other Devil's name?
Faith, here's an equivocator, that could swear in both
the scales against either scale, who committed treason
enough for God's sake, yet could not equivocate to   10
Heaven: O, come in, equivocator.   [*Knocking.*
Knock, knock, knock! Who's there? Faith, here's an
English tailor come hither, for stealing out of a French
hose: come in, tailor, here you may roast your goose.
                                         [*Knocking.*
Knock, knock! Never at quiet! What are you? But this
place is too cold for Hell. I'll Devil-porter it no further:
I had thought to have let in some of all professions, that
go the primrose way to th'everlasting bonfire.
                                         [*Knocking.*
Anon, anon! I pray you, remember the porter.[47]
                                    [*He opens the gate.*

Enter MACDUFF *and* LENNOX.

MACDUFF   Was it so late, friend, ere you went to bed, that you do   20
lie so late?
PORTER   Faith, sir, we were carousing till the second cock;[48]
and drink, sir, is a great provoker of three things.
MACDUFF   What three things does drink especially provoke?
PORTER   Marry, sir, nose-painting, sleep, and urine. Lechery, sir,
it provokes and unprovokes: it provokes the desire, but
it takes away the performance. Therefore, much drink

may be said to be an equivocator with lechery: it makes
him, and it mars him; it sets him on, and it takes him
off; it persuades him, and disheartens him; makes him   30
stand to, and not stand to: in conclusion, equivocates
him in a sleep, and, giving him the lie, leaves him.[49]

MACDUFF I believe drink gave thee the lie last night.

PORTER That it did, sir, i'the very throat on me: but I requited
him for his lie, and (I think) being too strong for him,
though he took up my legs sometime, yet I made a
shift to cast him.[50]

MACDUFF Is thy master stirring?

Enter MACBETH, *in a dressing-gown.*

Our knocking has awaked him; here he comes.

[Exit porter.

LENNOX Good–morrow, noble sir.

MACBETH   Good–morrow, both.   40

MACDUFF Is the King stirring, worthy Thane?

MACBETH   Not yet.

MACDUFF He did command me to call timely on him;
I have almost slipped the hour.

MACBETH   I'll bring you to him.

[They move towards an inner door.

MACDUFF I know this is a joyful trouble to you;
But yet 'tis one.

MACBETH The labour we delight in physics pain.
This is the door.

MACDUFF   I'll make so bold to call,
For 'tis my limited service.   *[Exit.*

LENNOX Goes the King hence today?

MACBETH He does: he did appoint so.   50

LENNOX The night has been unruly: where we lay,
Our chimneys were blown down, and (as they say)
Lamentings heard i'th'air, strange screams of death,
And prophesying with accents terrible
Of dire combustion and confused events
New hatched to th'woeful time. The obscure bird [51]
Clamoured the livelong night; some say, the earth
Was feverous and did shake.

MACBETH   'Twas a rough night.

LENNOX My young remembrance cannot parallel
A fellow to it.   60

Enter MACDUFF.

MACDUFF O horror, horror, horror! Tongue, nor heart,
Cannot conceive nor name thee!

MACBETH, LENNOX   What's the matter?

MACDUFF Confusion now hath made his masterpiece:
Most sacrilegious murther hath broke ope
The Lord's anointed temple,[52] and stole thence
The life o'th'building.

MACBETH   What is't you say? The life?

LENNOX Mean you his Majesty?

MACDUFF Approach the chamber, and destroy your sight
With a new Gorgon. Do not bid me speak;
See, and then speak yourselves. [*Exeunt Macbeth, Lennox.*
                              – Awake, awake!   70
Ring the alarum-bell! Murther and treason!
Banquo and Donalbain! Malcolm, awake!
Shake off this downy sleep, death's counterfeit,
And look on death itself! Up, up, and see
The great doom's image![53] Malcolm, Banquo,
As from your graves rise up, and walk like sprites,
To countenance this horror! Ring the bell! [*Bell rings.*

Enter LADY MACBETH, *in a dressing-gown.*

LADY M. What's the business,
That such a hideous trumpet calls to parley
The sleepers of the house? Speak, speak!

MACDUFF   O gentle lady, 80
'Tis not for you to hear what I can speak:
The repetition, in a woman's ear,
Would murther as it fell.

Enter BANQUO.

                              O Banquo, Banquo,
Our royal master's murthered!

LADY M.   Woe, alas!
What, in our house?

BANQUO   Too cruel, anywhere.
– Dear Duff, I prithee contradict thyself,

And say it is not so.

Enter MACBETH, LENNOX *and* ROSS.

MACBETH Had I but died an hour before this chance,
I had lived a blessèd time; for, from this instant,
There's nothing serious in mortality: 90
All is but toys; renown and grace is dead;
The wine of life is drawn, and the mere lees
Is left this vault to brag of.

Enter MALCOLM *and* DONALBAIN.

DONALB. What is amiss?
MACBETH You are, and do not know't:
The spring, the head, the fountain of your blood
Is stopped; the very source of it is stopped.
MACDUFF Your royal father's murthered.
MALCOLM O, by whom?
LENNOX Those of his chamber, as it seemed, had done't:
Their hands and faces were all badged with blood;
So were their daggers, which, unwiped, we found 100
Upon their pillows. They stared and were distracted;
No man's life was to be trusted with them.
MACBETH O, yet I do repent me of my fury,
That I did kill them.
MACDUFF Wherefore did you so?
MACBETH Who can be wise, amazed, temp'rate and furious,
Loyal and neutral, in a moment? No man:
Th'expedition of my violent love
Outrun the pauser, reason. Here lay Duncan,
His silver skin laced with his golden blood,
And his gashed stabs looked like a breach in nature 110
For ruin's wasteful entrance; there, the murtherers,
Steeped in the colours of their trade, their daggers
Unmannerly breeched with gore: who could refrain,
That had a heart to love, and in that heart
Courage to make's love known?
LADY M. Help me hence, ho!
MACDUFF Look to the lady.
MALCOLM [*aside to Donalbain:*] Why do we hold our tongues,
That most may claim this argument for ours?

DONALB. [*aside to Malcolm:*] What should be spoken here, where
                                                     our fate,
       Hid in an auger-hole, may rush and seize us?[54]
       Let's away. Our tears are not yet brewed.   120
MALCOLM [*aside to him:*] Nor our strong sorrow upon the foot
                                                  of motion.[55]
BANQUO Look to the lady;   [*Exit Lady Macbeth, aided.*
       And when we have our naked frailties hid,
       That suffer in exposure,[56] let us meet,
       And question this most bloody piece of work,
       To know it further. Fears and scruples shake us:
       In the great hand of God I stand, and thence
       Against the undivulged pretence I fight
       Of treasonous malice.
MACDUFF   And so do I.
ALL   So all.
MACBETH Let's briefly put on manly readiness.   130
       And meet i'th'hall together.
ALL   Well contented.
             [*Exeunt all except Malcolm and Donalbain.*
MALCOLM What will you do? Let's not consort with them:
       To show an unfelt sorrow is an office
       Which the false man does easy. I'll to England.
DONALB. To Ireland, I: our separated fortune
       Shall keep us both the safer. Where we are
       There's daggers in men's smiles: the near in blood,
       The nearer bloody.[57]
MALCOLM   This murtherous shaft that's shot
       Hath not yet lighted, and our safest way
       Is to avoid the aim. Therefore to horse,   140
       And let us not be dainty of leave-taking,
       But shift away: there's warrant in that theft
       Which steals itself when there's no mercy left.[58]
                          [*Exeunt.*

SCENE 4.

Near Macbeth's castle.

Enter ROSS *with an* OLD MAN.

OLD MAN Threescore and ten I can remember well,
    Within the volume of which time I have seen
    Hours dreadful and things strange; but this sore night
    Hath trifled former knowings.

ROSS   Ha, good father,
    Thou seest the heavens, as troubled with man's act,
    Threatens his bloody stage: by th'clock 'tis day,
    And yet dark night strangles the travelling lamp:
    Is't night's predominance, or the day's shame,
    That darkness does the face of earth entomb,
    When living light should kiss it?

OLD MAN   'Tis unnatural,   10
    Even like the deed that's done. On Tuesday last,
    A falcon, tow'ring in her pride of place,
    Was by a mousing owl hawked at and killed.

ROSS And Duncan's horses (a thing most strange and
                   certain)
    Beauteous and swift, the minions of their race,
    Turned wild in nature, broke their stalls, flung out,
    Contending 'gainst obedience, as they would
    Make war with mankind.

OLD MAN   'Tis said they ate each other.

ROSS They did so, to th'amazement of mine eyes,
    That looked upon't.

Enter MACDUFF.

        Here comes the good Macduff. 20
    – How goes the world, sir, now?

MACDUFF   Why, see you not?

ROSS Is't known who did this more than bloody deed?

MACDUFF Those that Macbeth hath slain.

ROSS   Alas the day;
    What good could they pretend?

MACDUFF   They were suborned.
Malcolm and Donalbain, the King's two sons,
Are stol'n away and fled, which puts upon them
Suspicion of the deed.

ROSS   'Gainst nature still:
Thriftless ambition, that wilt raven up
Thine own life's means! Then 'tis most like
The sovereignty will fall upon Macbeth.[59]   30

MACDUFF He is already named, and gone to Scone
To be invested.

ROSS   Where is Duncan's body?

MACDUFF Carried to Colmekill,[60]
The sacred storehouse of his predecessors,
And guardian of their bones.

ROSS   Will you to Scone?

MACDUFF No cousin, I'll to Fife.

ROSS   Well, I will thither.

MACDUFF Well, may you see things well done there (adieu),
Lest our old robes sit easier than our new.

ROSS Farewell, father.

OLD MAN God's benison go with you, and with those   40
That would make good of bad, and friends of foes!
                            [*Exeunt.*

ACT 3, SCENE 1.

A hall in the palace at Forres.

Enter BANQUO.

BANQUO   Thou hast it now, King, Cawdor, Glamis, all,
          As the Weyard Women promised, and I fear
          Thou play'dst most foully for't; yet it was said
          It should not stand in thy posterity,
          But that myself should be the root and father
          Of many kings. If there come truth from them
          (As upon thee, Macbeth, their speeches shine),
          Why, by the verities on thee made good,
          May they not be my oracles as well,
          And set me up in hope? But hush, no more.   10

Sennet sounds. Enter MACBETH *as King,* LADY MACBETH
as Queen, LENNOX, ROSS, LORDS *and* ATTENDANTS.

MACBETH   Here's our chief guest.
LADY M.   If he had been forgotten,
          It had been as a gap in our great feast,
          And all-thing unbecoming.
MACBETH   Tonight we hold a solemn supper, sir,
          And I'll request your presence.
BANQUO   Let your Highness
          Command upon me, to the which my duties
          Are with a most indíssoluble tie
          For ever knit.
MACBETH   Ride you this afternoon?
BANQUO   Ay, my good lord.
MACBETH   We should have else desired your good advice   20
          (Which still hath been both grave and prosperous)
          In this day's council; but we'll take tomorrow.[61]
          Is't far you ride?
BANQUO   As far, my lord, as will fill up the time
          'Twixt this and supper. Go not my horse the better,

I must become a borrower of the night
For a dark hour or twain.

MACBETH   Fail not our feast.
BANQUO   My lord, I will not.
MACBETH   We hear our bloody cousins are bestowed
In England and in Ireland, not confessing   30
Their cruel parricide, filling their hearers
With strange invention. But of that tomorrow,
When therewithal we shall have cause of state
Craving us jointly. Hie you to horse: adieu,
Till you return at night. Goes Fleance with you?
BANQUO   Ay, my good lord: our time does call upon's.
MACBETH   I wish your horses swift and sure of foot;
And so I do commend you to their backs.
Farewell.   [Exit Banquo.
Let every man be master of his time   40
Till seven at night; to make society
The sweeter welcome, we will keep ourself
Till supper-time alone: while then, God be with you!
          [Exeunt all except Macbeth and an attendant.
Sirrah, a word with you. Attend those men
Our pleasure?
ATTEND.   They are, my lord, without the palace gate.
MACBETH   Bring them before us.   [Exit attendant.
                    To be thus is nothing,
But to be safely thus. Our fears in Banquo
Stick deep, and in his royalty of nature
Reigns that which would be feared. 'Tis much
                                    he dares,   50
And, to that dauntless temper of his mind,
He hath a wisdom that doth guide his valour
To act in safety. There is none but he
Whose being I do fear; and under him
My Genius is rebuked, as it is said
Mark Antony's was by Cæsar.[62] He chid the Sisters,
When first they put the name of king upon me,
And bade them speak to him; then, prophet-like,
They hailed him father to a line of kings.
Upon my head they placed a fruitless crown,   60

And put a barren sceptre in my gripe,
Thence to be wrenched with an unlineal hand,
No son of mine succeeding. If't be so,
For Banquo's issue have I filed my mind,
For them the gracious Duncan have I murthered,
Put rancours in the vessel of my peace
Only for them, and mine eternal jewel
Given to the common enemy of man,[63]
To make them kings, the seeds of Banquo kings!
Rather than so, come Fate into the list,   70
And champion me to th'utterance.[64] – Who's there?

Enter the ATTENDANT *with* TWO MURDERERS.

[*To attendant:*] Now go to the door, and stay there till
                                                    we call.
                                            [*Exit attendant.*

– Was it not yesterday we spoke together?

MURD. 1   It was, so please your Highness.

MACBETH   Well then, now
Have you considered of my speeches? Know
That it was he, in the times past, which held you
So under fortune, which you thought had been
Our innocent self. This I made good to you
In our last conference; passed in probation with you,
How you were borne in hand, how crossed,
                                      the instruments,   80
Who wrought with them, and all things else that might
To half a soul and to a notion crazed
Say 'Thus did Banquo'.

MURD. 1   You made it known to us.

MACBETH   I did so; and went further, which is now
Our point of second meeting. Do you find
Your patience so predominant in your nature,
That you can let this go? Are you so gospelled,
To pray for this good man, and for his issue,
Whose heavy hand hath bowed you to the grave
And beggared yours for ever?

MURD. 1   We are men, my liege.   90

MACBETH   Ay, in the catalogue ye go for men,

As hounds and greyhounds, mongrels, spaniels, curs,
Shoughs, water-rugs and demi-wolves are clept
All by the name of dogs. The valued file
Distinguishes the swift, the slow, the subtle,
The housekeeper, the hunter, every one
According to the gift which bounteous nature
Hath in him closed, whereby he does receive
Particular addition, from the bill
That writes them all alike; and so of men.   100
Now, if you have a station in the file,
Not i'th'worst rank of manhood, say't,
And I will put that business in your bosoms,
Whose execution takes your enemy off,
Grapples you to the heart and love of us,
Who wear our health but sickly in his life,
Which in his death were perfect.

MURD. 2   I am one, my liege,
Whom the vile blows and buffets of the world
Hath so incensed, that I am reckless what
I do to spite the world.

MURD. 1   And I another,   110
So weary with disasters, tugged with fortune,
That I would set my life on any chance,
To mend it or be rid on't.

MACBETH   Both of you
Know Banquo was your enemy.

BOTH   True, my lord.

MACBETH So is he mine; and in such bloody distance
That every minute of his being thrusts
Against my near'st of life; and though I could
With barefaced power sweep him from my sight
And bid my will avouch it, yet I must not,
For certain friends that are both his and mine,   120
Whose loves I may not drop, but wail his fall
Who I myself struck down; and thence it is
That I to your assistance do make love,
Masking the business from the common eye,
For sundry weighty reasons.

MURD. 2   We shall, my lord,

Perform what you command us.

MURD. 1   Though our lives —

MACBETH Your spirits shine through you. Within this hour at most,
I will advise you where to plant yourselves,
Acquaint you with the perfect spy o'th'time,[65]
The moment on't, for't must be done tonight,   130
And something from the palace; always thought
That I require a clearness; and with him,
To leave no rubs nor botches in the work,
Fleance his son, that keeps him company,
Whose absence is no less material to me
Than is his father's, must embrace the fate
Of that dark hour. Resolve yourselves apart;
I'll come to you anon.

BOTH   We are resolved, my lord.

MACBETH I'll call upon you straight: abide within.
It is concluded. — Banquo, thy soul's flight,   140
If it find Heaven, must find it out tonight.

                                            [Exeunt.

SCENE 2.

Inside the palace at Forres.

Enter LADY MACBETH *(as Queen) and a* SERVANT.

LADY M.   Is Banquo gone from court?
SERVANT   Ay, madam, but returns again tonight.
LADY M.   Say to the King, I would attend his leisure
For a few words.
SERVANT   Madam, I will.   [*Exit.*
LADY M.   Nought's had, all's spent,
Where our desire is got without content:
'Tis safer to be that which we destroy,
Than by destruction dwell in doubtful joy.

                        Enter MACBETH.

How now, my lord? Why do you keep alone,   10
Of sorriest fancies your companions making,
Using those thoughts which should indeed have died

            With them they think on? Things without all remedy
            Should be without regard: what's done, is done.
MACBETH   We have scorched the snake, not killed it:
            She'll close and be herself, whilst our poor malice
            Remains in danger of her former tooth.
            But let the frame of things disjoint,
            Both the worlds suffer,[66]
            Ere we will eat our meal in fear, and sleep   20
            In the affliction of these terrible dreams
            That shake us nightly. Better be with the dead,
            Whom we, to gain our peace, have sent to peace,
            Than on the torture of the mind to lie
            In restless ecstasy.
            Duncan is in his grave:
            After life's fitful fever, he sleeps well;
            Treason has done his worst: nor steel, nor poison,
            Malice domestic, foreign levy, nothing,
            Can touch him further.   30
LADY M.   Come on:
            Gentle my lord, sleek o'er your rugged looks,
            Be bright and jovial among your guests tonight.
MACBETH   So shall I, love, and so, I pray, be you.
            Let your remembrance apply to Banquo:
            Present him eminence, both with eye and tongue;
            Unsafe the while, that we
            Must lave our honours in these flattering streams,
            And make our faces vizards to our hearts,
            Disguising what they are.
LADY M.   You must leave this.   40
MACBETH   O, full of scorpions is my mind, dear wife!
            Thou know'st that Banquo and his Fleance lives.
LADY M.   But in them nature's copy's not eterne.
MACBETH   There's comfort yet: they are assailable.
            Then be thou jocund: ere the bat hath flown
            His cloistered flight, ere to black Heccat's summons
            The shard-borne beetle with his drowsy hums
            Hath rung night's yawning peal, there shall be done
            A deed of dreadful note.[67]
LADY M.   What's to be done?

MACBETH Be innocent of the knowledge, dearest chuck,   50
         Till thou applaud the deed. – Come, seeling night,
         Scarf up the tender eye of pitiful day,
         And with thy bloody and invisible hand
         Cancel and tear to pieces that great bond
         Which keeps me pale! Light thickens, and the crow
         Makes wing to th'rooky wood:[68]
         Good things of day begin to droop and drowse,
         Whiles night's black agents to their preys do rouse.
         Thou marvell'st at my words; but hold thee still:
         Things bad begun make strong themselves by ill.   60
         So prithee go with me.

                                                      [*Exeunt.*

                              SCENE 3.

                        Nightfall. A pathway.

                    Enter THREE MURDERERS.

MURD. 1 But who did bid thee join with us?
MURD. 3   Macbeth.
MURD. 2 [*to Murderer 1:*] He needs not our mistrust, since he delivers
         Our offices and what we have to do,
         To the direction just.[69]
MURD. 1 [*to Murderer 3:*]   Then stand with us.
         The west yet glimmers with some streaks of day.
         Now spurs the lated traveller apace
         To gain the timely inn, and near approaches
         The subject of our watch.
MURD. 3   Hark! I hear horses.
BANQUO   [*within:*] Give us a light there, ho!
MURD. 2   Then 'tis he; the rest
         That are within the note of expectation   10
         Already are i'th'court.
MURD. 1   His horses go about.
MURD. 3 Almost a mile; but he does usually
         (So all men do) from hence to th'palace gate
         Make it their walk.

       Enter FLEANCE *(holding a burning torch) and* BANQUO.

MURD. 2	A light, a light!
MURD. 3	'Tis he.
MURD. 1	Stand to't.
BANQUO	It will be rain tonight.
MURD. 1	Let it come down!

[*Murderer 1 strikes out the torch; the others attack Banquo.*

BANQUO   O, treachery! – Fly, good Fleance, fly, fly, fly!
Thou mayst revenge. – O slave!

[*He dies; Fleance escapes.*

MURD. 3   Who did strike out the light?
MURD. 1   Was't not the way?
MURD. 3   There's but one down; the son is fled.
MURD. 2   We have lost   20
Best half of our affair.
MURD. 1   Well, let's away, and say how much is done.

[*Exeunt.*

SCENE 4.

The hall of the palace at Forres. A banquet has been prepared.

Enter MACBETH, LADY MACBETH,
ROSS, LENNOX, LORDS, *and* ATTENDANTS.

MACBETH   You know your own degrees; sit down. At first
And last, the hearty welcome.
LORDS   Thanks to your Majesty.

Lady Macbeth sits on her throne. The guests sit at the table.

MACBETH   Ourself will mingle with society,
And play the humble host;
Our hostess keeps her state, but in best time
We will require her welcome.
LADY M.   Pronounce it for me, sir, to all our friends,
For my heart speaks they are welcome.

Enter MURDERER 1 *as the guests acknowledge the welcome.*

MACBETH   See, they encounter thee with their hearts' thanks.
Both sides are even: here I'll sit i'th'midst.   10
[*To lords:*] Be large in mirth, anon we'll drink a measure
The table round.

[*He talks aside with Murderer 1.*]
                              There's blood upon thy face.

MURD.   'Tis Banquo's then.

MACBETH   'Tis better thee without than he within.[70]
          Is he dispatched?

MURD.   My lord, his throat is cut: that I did for him.

MACBETH   Thou art the best o'th'cut-throats! Yet he's good
          That did the like for Fleance: if thou didst it,
          Thou art the nonpareil.

MURD.   Most royal sir,
          Fleance is scaped.   20

MACBETH   Then comes my fit again: I had else been perfect;
          Whole as the marble, founded as the rock,
          As broad and general as the casing air;
          But now I am cabined, cribbed, confined, bound in
          To saucy doubts and fears. But Banquo's safe?

MURD.   Ay, my good lord: safe in a ditch he bides,
          With twenty trenchèd gashes on his head;
          The least a death to nature.

MACBETH   Thanks for that:
          There the grown serpent lies; the worm that's fled
          Hath nature that in time will venom breed,   30
          No teeth for th'present. Get thee gone; tomorrow
          We'll hear, ourselves, again.   [*Exit murderer.*

LADY M.   My royal lord,
          You do not give the cheer. The feast is sold
          That is not often vouched, while 'tis a-making,
          'Tis given with welcome: to feed were best at home;
          From thence the sauce to meat is ceremony;
          Meeting were bare without it.[71]

          Enter BANQUO'S GHOST. *It sits in Macbeth's place.*

MACBETH   [*to Lady Macbeth:*]   Sweet remembrancer!
          [*To lords:*] Now good digestion wait on appetite,
          And health on both!

LENNOX   May't please your Highness sit?

MACBETH   Here had we now our country's honour roofed,   40
          Were the graced person of our Banquo present,
          Who may I rather challenge for unkindness

Than pity for mischance.

ROSS   His absence, sir,
Lays blame upon his promise. Please't your Highness
To grace us with your royal company?

MACBETH The table's full.

LENNOX   Here is a place reserved, sir.

MACBETH Where?

LENNOX Here, my good lord. What is't that moves your Highness?

MACBETH Which of you have done this?

LORDS   What, my good lord?

MACBETH [*to Ghost:*] Thou canst not say I did it: never shake   50
Thy gory locks at me.

ROSS Gentlemen, rise: his Highness is not well.   [*Guests rise.*

LADY M. Sit, worthy friends: my lord is often thus,
And hath been from his youth. Pray you, keep seat:
The fit is momentary; upon a thought
He will again be well. If much you note him,
You shall offend him and extend his passion.
Feed, and regard him not.
[*She speaks aside with Macbeth:*] Are you a man?

MACBETH Ay, and a bold one, that dare look on that
Which might appal the Devil.

LADY M.   O proper stuff!   60
This is the very painting of your fear:
This is the air-drawn dagger which, you said,
Led you to Duncan. O, these flaws and starts
(Impostors to true fear) would well become
A woman's story at a winter's fire,
Authorized by her grandam. Shame itself.
Why do you make such faces? When all's done,
You look but on a stool.

MACBETH Prithee, see there! Behold, look, lo! [*To Ghost:*] How
                                                   say you?

Why, what care I if thou canst nod? Speak too.   70
If charnel-houses and our graves must send
Those that we bury back, our monuments
Shall be the maws of kites.[72]   [*Exit Ghost.*

LADY M. What, quite unmanned in folly?

MACBETH If I stand here, I saw him.

LADY M.   Fie, for shame!
MACBETH Blood hath been shed ere now, i'th'olden time,
Ere human statute purged the gentle weal;[73]
Ay, and since too, murthers have been performed
Too terrible for the ear. The time has been,
That, when the brains were out, the man would die,   80
And there an end; but now they rise again,
With twenty mortal murthers on their crowns,
And push us from our stools. This is more strange
Than such a murther is.
LADY M.   My worthy lord,
Your noble friends do lack you.
MACBETH   I do forget.
– Do not muse at me, my most worthy friends;
I have a strange infirmity, which is nothing
To those that know me. Come, love and health to all;
Then I'll sit down. – Give me some wine, fill full. –

        Enter BANQUO'S GHOST, *unseen by Macbeth.*

I drink to th'general joy o'th'whole table,   90
And to our dear friend Banquo, whom we miss;
Would he were here! To all, and him, we thirst,
And all to all!
LORDS   Our duties, and the pledge!
MACBETH [*seeing Ghost:*] Avaunt, and quit my sight! Let the
                                              earth hide thee!
Thy bones are marrowless, thy blood is cold;
Thou hast no speculation in those eyes
Which thou dost glare with!
LADY M.   Think of this, good peers,
But as a thing of custom: 'tis no other;
Only it spoils the pleasure of the time.
MACBETH [*to Ghost:*] What man dare, I dare: 100
Approach thou like the rugged Russian bear,
The armed rhinoceros, or th'Hyrcan tiger,
Take any shape but that, and my firm nerves
Shall never tremble. Or be alive again,
And dare me to the desert with thy sword:
If trembling I inhabit then, protest me

The baby of a girl.[74] Hence, horrible shadow!
Unreal mock'ry, hence!   [*Exit Ghost.*
                          Why, so; being gone,
I am a man again. [*To guests:*] Pray you, sit still.

LADY M.   You have displaced the mirth, broke the good meeting,   110
With most admired disorder.

MACBETH   Can such things be,
And overcome us like a summer's cloud,
Without our special wonder? You make me strange
Even to the disposition that I owe,
When now I think you can behold such sights,
And keep the natural ruby of your cheeks,
When mine is blanched with fear.

ROSS   What sights, my lord?

LADY M.   I pray you, speak not: he grows worse and worse;
Question enrages him. At once, good night.
Stand not upon the order of your going,   120
But go at once.

LENNOX   Good night, and better health
Attend his Majesty!

LADY M.   A kind good night to all!
                          [*Exeunt guests and attendants.*

MACBETH   It will have blood, they say: blood will have blood.
Stones have been known to move, and trees to speak;
Augures and understood relations have
By maggot-pies and choughs and rooks brought forth
The secret'st man of blood.[75] What is the night?

LADY M.   Almost at odds with morning, which is which.

MACBETH   How say'st thou, that Macduff denies his person
At our great bidding?

LADY M.   Did you send to him, sir?   130

MACBETH   I hear it by the way; but I will send:
There's not a one of them but in his house
I keep a servant fee'd. I will tomorrow
(And betimes I will) to the Weyard Sisters.
More shall they speak: for now I am bent to know,
By the worst means, the worst. For mine own good,
All causes shall give way. I am in blood
Stepped in so far that, should I wade no more,

Returning were as tedious as go o'er:
Strange things I have in head that will to hand,   140
Which must be acted ere they may be scanned.
LADY M.   You lack the season of all natures, sleep.
MACBETH   Come, we'll to sleep. My strange and self abuse
Is the initiate fear that wants hard use:[76]
We are yet but young in deed.   [Exeunt.

SCENE 5.

A heath. Thunder.

Enter the THREE WITCHES, *meeting* HECCAT.

WITCH I   Why, how now, Heccat? You look angerly.
HECCAT   Have I not reason, beldams, as you are
Saucy and overbold? How did you dare
To trade and traffic with Macbeth
In riddles and affairs of death;
And I, the mistress of your charms,
The close contriver of all harms,
Was never called to bear my part,
Or show the glory of our art?
And, which is worse, all you have done   10
Hath been but for a wayward son,
Spiteful and wrathful, who (as others do)
Loves for his own ends, not for you.
But make amends now: get you gone,
And, at the Pit of Acheron,
Meet me i'th'morning: thither he
Will come, to know his destiny.
Your vessels and your spells provide,
Your charms and every thing beside.
I am for th'air; this night I'll spend   20
Unto a dismal and a fatal end.
Great business must be wrought ere noon.
Upon the corner of the moon,
There hangs a vap'rous drop profound:
I'll catch it ere it come to ground;
And that, distilled by magic sleights,

Shall raise such artificial sprites
As by the strength of their illusion
Shall draw him on to his confusion.
He shall spurn fate, scorn death, and bear   30
His hopes 'bove wisdom, grace, and fear:
And you all know, security
Is mortals' chiefest enemy.

Music. Enter SPIRITS *above.*
They begin the song 'Come away, come away'.[77]

HECCAT   Hark, I am called: my little spirit, see,
Sits in a foggy cloud, and stays for me.

The spirits continue the song. Exit Heccat.
The song and music end. Exeunt spirits.

WITCH I   Come, let's make haste; she'll soon be back again.

[*Exeunt.*

SCENE 6.

A location in Scotland.

Enter LENNOX *and another* LORD.

LENNOX   My former speeches have but hit your thoughts,
Which can interpret farther; only I say
Things have been strangely borne. The gracious Duncan
Was pitied of Macbeth: marry, he was dead;
And the right valiant Banquo walked too late,
Whom you may say (if't please you) Fleance killed,
For Fleance fled: men must not walk too late.
Who cannot want the thought, how monstrous
It was for Malcolm and for Donalbain
To kill their gracious father? Damnèd fact: 10
How it did grieve Macbeth! Did he not straight,
In pious rage, the two delinquents tear,
That were the slaves of drink and thralls of sleep?
Was not that nobly done? Ay, and wisely too;
For 'twould have angered any heart alive
To hear the men deny't. So that, I say,
He has borne all things well; and I do think

That, had he Duncan's sons under his key
(As, and't please Heaven, he shall not), they should find
What 'twere to kill a father; so should Fleance.   20
But peace; for from broad words, and 'cause he failed
His presence at the tyrant's feast, I hear,
Macduff lives in disgrace. Sir, can you tell
Where he bestows himself?

LORD   The son of Duncan
(From whom this tyrant holds the due of birth)
Lives in the English court, and is received
Of the most pious Edward with such grace
That the malevolence of fortune nothing
Takes from his high respect.[78] Thither Macduff
Is gone, to pray the holy King, upon his aid   30
To wake Northumberland and warlike Seyward,
That by the help of these (with Him above
To ratify the work) we may again
Give to our tables meat, sleep to our nights;
Free, from our feasts and banquets, bloody knives;
Do faithful homage and receive free honours:
All which we pine for now. And this report
Hath so exasperate the King that he
Prepares for some attempt of war.

LENNOX   Sent he to Macduff?

LORD   He did, and with an absolute 'Sir, not I',   40
The cloudy messenger turns me his back,[79]
And hums, as who should say, 'You'll rue the time
That clogs me with this answer.'

LENNOX   And that well might
Advise him to a caution, t'hold what distance
His wisdom can provide. Some holy angel
Fly to the court of England and unfold
His message ere he come, that a swift blessing
May soon return to this, our suffering country
Under a hand accurs'd!

LORD   I'll send my prayers with him.   50

                                        [*Exeunt.*

ACT 4, SCENE 1.

The Pit of Acheron, where a cauldron stands. Thunder.

Enter the THREE WITCHES.

WITCH 1   Thrice the brinded cat hath mewed.
WITCH 2   Thrice, and once the hedge–pig whined.
WITCH 3   Harpier cries; 'tis time, 'tis time.

                                  [*They circle the cauldron.*

WITCH 1   Round about the cauldron go;
          In, the poisoned entrails throw.
          Toad, that under cold stone,
          Days and nights has thirty–one,
          Sweltered venom sleeping got,
          Boil thou first i'th'charmèd pot.
ALL   Double, double, toil and trouble;   10
          Fire burn, and cauldron bubble.
WITCH 2   Fillet of a fenny snake
          In the cauldron boil and bake;
          Eye of newt and toe of frog,
          Wool of bat and tongue of dog,
          Adder's fork and blind–worm's sting,
          Lizard's leg and howlet's wing;
          For a charm of pow'rful trouble,
          Like a Hell–broth, boil and bubble.
ALL   Double, double, toil and trouble;   20
          Fire burn, and cauldron bubble.
WITCH 3   Scale of dragon, tooth of wolf,
          Witches' mummy, maw and gulf
          Of the ravined salt–sea shark,
          Root of hemlock digged i'th'dark,
          Liver of blaspheming Jew,
          Gall of goat, and slips of yew
          Slivered in the moon's eclipse,
          Nose of Turk, and Tartar's lips,
          Finger of birth–strangled babe   30
          Ditch–delivered by a drab:
          Make the gruel thick and slab.

Add thereto a tiger's chaudron,
For th'ingredience of our cauldron.

ALL   Double, double, toil and trouble;
Fire burn, and cauldron bubble.

WITCH 2   Cool it with a báboon's blood;
Then the charm is firm and good.

         Enter HECCAT *and* THREE MORE WITCHES.

HECCAT   O, well done! I commend your pains,
And everyone shall share i'th'gains;   40
And now about the cauldron sing,
Like elves and fairies in a ring,
Enchanting all that you put in.

        Music and song: 'Black spirits', etc.[80]

WITCH 2   By the pricking of my thumbs,
Something wicked this way comes: [*Knocking heard.*
Open, locks,
Whoever knocks!

           Enter MACBETH.

MACBETH   How now, you secret, black and midnight hags?
What is't you do?

ALL   A deed without a name.

MACBETH   I conjure you, by that which you profess   50
(Howe'er you come to know it): answer me.
Though you untie the winds, and let them fight
Against the churches; though the yesty waves
Confound and swallow navigation up;
Though bladed corn be lodged and trees blown down;
Though castles topple on their warders' heads;
Though palaces and pyramids do slope
Their heads to their foundations; though the treasure
Of Nature's germens tumble altogether,
Even till destruction sicken: answer me   60
To what I ask you.

WITCH 1   Speak.

WITCH 2   Demand.

WITCH 3   We'll answer.

WITCH 1   Say if th'hadst rather hear it from *our* mouths,
Or from our masters'.

MACBETH   Call 'em: let me see 'em!

WITCH I   Pour in sow's blood, that hath eaten
Her nine farrow; grease, that's sweaten
From the murderer's gibbet, throw
Into the flame.

ALL   Come high or low:
Thyself and office deftly show.

Thunder. The FIRST APPARITION, *a helmeted head,*
rises into sight.[81]

MACBETH Tell me, thou unknown power –

WITCH I   He knows thy thought:
Hear his speech, but say thou nought.   70

APPAR. I Macbeth, Macbeth, Macbeth! Beware Macduff;
Beware the Thane of Fife. Dismiss me. Enough.
                              [It descends.

MACBETH Whate'er thou art, for thy good caution, thanks;
Thou hast harped my fear aright. But one word more –

WITCH I   He will not be commanded. Here's another,
More potent than the first.

Thunder. The SECOND APPARITION, *a blood-stained child,*
rises into sight.[82]

APPAR. 2 Macbeth, Macbeth, Macbeth!

MACBETH Had I three ears, I'd hear thee.

APPAR. 2 Be bloody, bold, and resolute: laugh to scorn
The power of man; for none of woman born   80
Shall harm Macbeth.   *[It descends.*

MACBETH Then live, Macduff: what need I fear of thee?
But yet I'll make assurance double sure,
And take a bond of fate: thou shalt not live,
That I may tell pale-hearted fear it lies,
And sleep in spite of thunder.

Thunder. The THIRD APPARITION, *a child crowned,*
with a tree in his hand, rises into sight.[83]

                             What is this,
That rises like the issue of a king,
And wears upon his baby-brow the round
And top of sovereignty?

ALL   Listen, but speak not to't.

APPAR. 3   Be lion-mettled, proud, and take no care   90
           Who chafes, who frets, or where conspirers are:
           Macbeth shall never vanquished be, until
           Great Birnam Wood to high Dunsinane Hill
           Shall come against him.   [*It descends.*
MACBETH   That will never be;
           Who can impress the forest, bid the tree
           Unfix his earth-bound root? Sweet bodements; good:
           Rebellious dead, rise never till the wood
           Of Birnam rise, and our high-placed Macbeth
           Shall live the lease of nature, pay his breath
           To time and mortal custom. Yet my heart   100
           Throbs to know one thing: tell me, if your art
           Can tell so much: shall Banquo's issue ever
           Reign in this kingdom?
ALL   Seek to know no more.
MACBETH   I will be satisfied. Deny me this,
           And an eternal curse fall on you! Let me know.
                    [*Hautboys play as the cauldron descends.*
           Why sinks that cauldron? And what noise is this?
WITCH 1   Show!
WITCH 2   Show!
WITCH 3   Show!
ALL   Show his eyes, and grieve his heart;   110
           Come like shadows, so depart.

           Enter a procession of EIGHT KINGS *(the last holding
                    a mirror) and* BANQUO'S GHOST.
                    Macbeth responds to each in turn.

MACBETH   Thou art too like the spirit of Banquo: down!
           Thy crown does sear mine eyeballs. And thy hair,
           Thou other gold-bound brow, is like the first;
           A third is like the former. – Filthy hags!
           Why do you show me this? – A fourth? Start, eyes!
           What, will the line stretch out to th'crack of Doom?
           Another yet? A seventh? I'll see no more.
           And yet the eighth appears, who bears a glass
           Which shows me many more; and some I see   120
           That two-fold balls and treble sceptres carry.

Horrible sight. Now I see 'tis true,
For the blood-boltered Banquo smiles upon me,
And points at them for his.   [*Procession departs.*
                              What, is this so?[84]

WITCH I   Ay sir, all this is so. But why
Stands Macbeth thus amazèdly?
Come, sisters, cheer we up his sprites,
And show the best of our delights.
I'll charm the air to give a sound,
While you perform your antic round: 130
That this great King may kindly say,
Our duties did his welcome pay.

Music. Witches dance. Music ends. All the witches and Heccat vanish.

MACBETH   Where are they? Gone? Let this pernicious hour
Stand aye accursèd in the calendar!
Come in, without there!

                    Enter LENNOX.

LENNOX   What's your Grace's will?
MACBETH   Saw you the Weyard Sisters?
LENNOX   No, my lord.
MACBETH   Came they not by you?
LENNOX   No indeed, my lord.
MACBETH   Infected be the air whereon they ride,
And damned all those that trust them! I did hear
The galloping of horse. Who was't came by?   140
LENNOX   'Tis two or three, my lord, that bring you word:
Macduff is fled to England.
MACBETH   Fled to England?
LENNOX   Ay, my good lord.
MACBETH   [*aside:*] Time, thou anticipat'st my dread exploits:
The flighty purpose never is o'ertook
Unless the deed go with it.[85] From this moment,
The very firstlings of my heart shall be
The firstlings of my hand. And even now,
To crown my thoughts with acts, be it thought and done:
The castle of Macduff I will surprise,   150
Seize upon Fife, give to th'edge o'th'sword
His wife, his babes, and all unfortunate souls

That trace him in his line. No boasting like a fool;
This deed I'll do before this purpose cool.
But no more sights. [*Aloud:*] Where are these gentlemen?
Come, bring me where they are.   [*Exeunt.*

SCENE 2.

Inside Macduff's castle in Fife.

Enter LADY MACDUFF, *her* SON, *and* ROSS.

LADY   What had he done, to make him fly the land?
ROSS   You must have patience, madam.
LADY   He had none:
His flight was madness: when our actions do not,
Our fears do make us traitors.
ROSS   You know not
Whether it was his wisdom or his fear.
LADY   'Wisdom'? To leave his wife, to leave his babes,
His mansion and his titles, in a place
From whence himself does fly? He loves us not;
He wants the natural touch: for the poor wren
(The most diminutive of birds) will fight,   10
Her young ones in her nest, against the owl.
All is the fear, and nothing is the love;
As little is the wisdom, where the flight
So runs against all reason.
ROSS   My dearest coz,
I pray you, school yourself. But, for your husband,
He is noble, wise, judicious, and best knows
The fits o'th'season. I dare not speak much further,
But cruel are the times, when we are traitors
And do not know ourselves; when we hold rumour
From what we fear, yet know not what we fear,   20
But float upon a wild and violent sea
Each way and move.[86] I take my leave of you;
Shall not be long but I'll be here again:
Things at the worst will cease, or else climb upward
To what they were before. – My pretty cousin,
Blessing upon you!

LADY	Fathered he is, and yet he's fatherless.
ROSS	I am so much a fool, should I stay longer,
	It would be my disgrace and your discomfort.
	I take my leave at once. [*Exit.*
LADY	Sirrah, your father's dead, 30
	And what will you do now? How will you live?
SON	As birds do, mother.
LADY	What, with worms and flies?
SON	With what I get, I mean, and so do they.
LADY	Poor bird! Thou'dst never fear the net nor lime,
	The pitfall nor the gin.
SON	Why should I, mother? Poor birds they are not set for.[87]
	My father is not dead, for all your saying.
LADY	Yes, he is dead. How wilt thou do for a father?
SON	Nay, how will you do for a husband?
LADY	Why, I can buy me twenty at any market. 40
SON	Then you'll buy 'em to sell again.
LADY	Thou speak'st with all thy wit, and yet i'faith
	With wit enough for thee.
SON	Was my father a traitor, mother?
LADY	Ay, that he was.
SON	What is a traitor?
LADY	Why, one that swears and lies.
SON	And be all traitors, that do so?
LADY	Every one that does so is a traitor, and must be hanged.
SON	And must they all be hanged that swear and lie? 50
LADY	Every one.
SON	Who must hang them?
LADY	Why, the honest men.
SON	Then the liars and swearers are fools; for there are liars and swearers enow to beat the honest men and hang up them.
LADY	Now God help thee, poor monkey! But how wilt thou do for a father?
SON	If he were dead, you'd weep for him; if you would not, it were a good sign that I should quickly have a 60 new father.
LADY	Poor prattler, how thou talk'st!

Enter a MESSENGER.

MESSENGER Bless you, fair dame! I am not to you known,
Though in your state of honour I am perfect.[88]
I doubt some danger does approach you nearly.
If you will take a homely man's advice,
Be not found here: hence, with your little ones.
To fright you thus, methinks I am too savage;
To do worse to you were fell cruelty,
Which is too nigh your person. Heaven preserve you!   70
I dare abide no longer.   [Exit.
LADY   Whither should I fly?
I have done no harm. But I remember now
I am in this earthly world, where to do harm
Is often laudable, to do good sometime
Accounted dangerous folly. Why then (alas)
Do I put up that womanly defence,
To say 'I have done no harm'?

                    Enter MURDERERS.

                            What are these faces?
MURD. I   Where is your husband?
LADY   I hope in no place so unsanctified   80
Where such as thou mayst find him.
MURD. I   He's a traitor.
SON   Thou liest, thou shag-eared villain.
MURD. I   What, you egg?
Young fry of treachery!   [He stabs the son.
SON   He has killed me, mother:
Run away, I pray you.   [He dies.
LADY   Murther!   [Exit Lady Macduff, pursued by the murderers.

                    SCENE 3.

England. Outside the palace of King Edward the Confessor.

                Enter MALCOLM and MACDUFF.

MALCOLM   Let us seek out some desolate shade, and there
Weep our sad bosoms empty.
MACDUFF   Let us rather
Hold fast the mortal sword, and, like good men,

Bestride our down-fall'n birthdom: each new morn
New widows howl, new orphans cry, new sorrows
Strike Heaven on the face, that it resounds
As if it felt with Scotland and yelled out
Like syllable of dolour.

MALCOLM   What I believe, I'll wail;
What know, believe; and what I can redress,
As I shall find the time to friend, I will.   10
What you have spoke, it may be so, perchance.
This tyrant, whose sole name blisters our tongues,
Was once thought honest: you have loved him well;
He hath not touched you yet. I am young, but something
You may discern of him through me;[89] and wisdom,
To offer up a weak, poor, innocent lamb,
T'appease an angry God.

MACDUFF   I am not treacherous.

MALCOLM   But Macbeth is.
A good and virtuous nature may recoil
In an imperial charge. But I shall crave your pardon: 20
That which you are, my thoughts cannot transpose;
Angels are bright still, though the brightest fell.[90]
Though all things foul would wear the brows of grace,
Yet grace must still look so.

MACDUFF   I have lost my hopes.

MALCOLM Perchance even there where I did find my doubts.
Why in that rawness left you wife and child,
Those precious motives, those strong knots of love,
Without leave-taking? I pray you,
Let not my jealousies be your dishonours,
But mine own safeties:[91] you may be rightly just,   30
Whatever I shall think.

MACDUFF   Bleed, bleed, poor country;
Great tyranny, lay thou thy basis sure,
For goodness dares not check thee: wear thou
                              thy wrongs;
The title is affeared.[92] Fare thee well, lord;
I would not be the villain that thou think'st
For the whole space that's in the tyrant's grasp
And the rich East to boot.

MALCOLM   Be not offended:
I speak not as in absolute fear of you.
I think our country sinks beneath the yoke,
It weeps, it bleeds, and each new day a gash   40
Is added to her wounds. I think, withal,
There would be hands uplifted in my right;
And here from gracious England have I offer
Of goodly thousands. But, for all this,
When I shall tread upon the tyrant's head,
Or wear it on my sword, yet my poor country
Shall have more vices that it had before,
More suffer, and more sundry ways than ever,
By him that shall succeed.

MACDUFF   What should he be?

MALCOLM It is myself I mean: in whom I know   50
All the particulars of vice so grafted
That, when they shall be opened, black Macbeth
Will seem as pure as snow, and the poor state
Esteem him as a lamb, being compared
With my confineless harms.

MACDUFF   Not in the legions
Of horrid Hell can come a devil more damned
In evils to top Macbeth.

MALCOLM   I grant him bloody,
Luxurious, avaricious, false, deceitful,
Sudden, malicious, smacking of every sin
That has a name. But there's no bottom, none,   60
In my voluptuousness: your wives, your daughters,
Your matrons, and your maids, could not fill up
The cistern of my lust, and my desire
All continent impediments would o'erbear
That did oppose my will. Better Macbeth,
Than such an one to reign.

MACDUFF   Boundless intemperance
In nature is a tyranny; it hath been
Th'untimely emptying of the happy throne,
And fall of many kings. But fear not yet
To take upon you what is yours: you may   70
Convey your pleasures in a spacious plenty,

And yet seem cold. The time you may so hoodwink:
We have willing dames enough; there cannot be
That vulture in you, to devour so many
As will to greatness dedicate themselves,
Finding it so inclined.

MALCOLM   With this, there grows,
In my most ill-composed affection, such
A stanchless avarice that, were I King,
I should cut off the nobles for their lands,
Desire his jewels and this other's house,   80
And my more-having would be as a sauce
To make me hunger more, that I should forge
Quarrels unjust against the good and loyal,
Destroying them for wealth.

MACDUFF   This avarice
Sticks deeper, grows with more pernicious root
Than summer-seeming lust; and it hath been
The sword of our slain kings; yet do not fear:
Scotland hath foisons to fill up your will
Of your mere own. All these are portable,
With other graces weighed.   90

MALCOLM But I have none. The king-becoming graces,
As justice, verity, temp'rance, stableness,
Bounty, perséverance, mercy, lowliness,
Devotion, patience, courage, fortitude,
I have no relish of them, but abound
In the division of each several crime,
Acting it many ways. Nay, had I power, I should
Pour the sweet milk of concord into Hell,
Uproot the universal peace, confound
All unity on earth.

MACDUFF   O Scotland, Scotland!   100

MALCOLM If such a one be fit to govern, speak.
I am as I have spoken.

MACDUFF   'Fit to govern'?
No, not to live! O nation miserable,
With an untitled tyrant, bloody-sceptred,
When shalt thou see thy wholesome days again,
Since that the truest issue of thy throne

By his own interdiction stands accurs'd,
And does blaspheme his breed? Thy royal father
Was a most sainted king; the Queen that bore thee,
Oft'ner upon her knees than on her feet,   110
Died every day she lived.[93] Fare thee well!
These evils thou repeat'st upon thyself
Hath banished me from Scotland. − O my breast,
Thy hope ends here!

MALCOLM   Macduff, this noble passion,
Child of integrity, hath from my soul
Wiped the black scruples, reconciled my thoughts
To thy good truth and honour. Devilish Macbeth,
By many of these trains, hath sought to win me
Into his power; and modest wisdom plucks me
From over-credulous haste; but God above   120
Deal between thee and me: for even now
I put myself to thy direction, and
Unspeak mine own detraction; here abjure
The taints and blames I laid upon myself,
For strangers to my nature. I am yet
Unknown to woman, never was forsworn,
Scarcely have coveted what was mine own,
At no time broke my faith, would not betray
The Devil to his fellow, and delight
No less in truth than life. My first false speaking   130
Was this upon myself. What I am truly
Is thine and my poor country's to command;
Whither indeed, before thy here-approach,
Old Seyward, with ten thousand warlike men,
Already at a point, was setting forth.
Now we'll together, and the chance of goodness
Be like our warranted quarrel![94] Why are you silent?

MACDUFF Such welcome and unwelcome things at once
'Tis hard to reconcile.

Enter a DOCTOR.

MALCOLM Well, more anon. − Comes the King forth, I pray you?   140
DOCTOR Ay, sir: there are a crew of wretched souls
That stay his cure: their malady convinces
The great assay of art; but, at his touch,

Such sanctity hath Heaven given his hand,
They presently amend.⁹⁵

MALCOLM   I thank you, doctor. [*Exit doctor.*

MACDUFF What's the disease he means?

MALCOLM   'Tis called 'The Evil'.
A most miraculous work in this good King,
Which often, since my here-remain in England,
I have seen him do: how he solicits Heaven,
Himself best knows; but strangely-visited people,   150
All swol'n and ulcerous, pitiful to the eye,
The mere despair of surgery, he cures,
Hanging a golden stamp about their necks,
Put on with holy prayers; and 'tis spoken,
To the succeeding royalty he leaves
The healing benediction. With this strange virtue,
He hath a heavenly gift of prophecy;
And sundry blessings hang about his throne
That speak him full of grace.

                        Enter ROSS.

MACDUFF   See who comes here.

MALCOLM My countryman; but yet I know him not.   160

MACDUFF – My ever gentle cousin, welcome hither.

MALCOLM I know him now. Good God, betimes remove
The means that makes us strangers!

ROSS   Sir, amen.

MACDUFF Stands Scotland where it did?

ROSS   Alas, poor country,
Almost afraid to know itself! It cannot
Be called our mother, but our grave; where nothing,
But who knows nothing, is once seen to smile;
Where sighs and groans, and shrieks that rend the air,
Are made, not marked; where violent sorrow seems
A modern ecstasy. The dead man's knell   170
Is there scarce asked 'For who?', and good men's lives
Expire before the flowers in their caps,
Dying or ere they sicken.

MACDUFF   O, relation
Too nice, and yet too true!

MALCOLM   What's the newest grief?

ROSS   That of an hour's age doth hiss the speaker;
          Each minute teems a new one.
MACDUFF   How does my wife?
ROSS   Why, well.
MACDUFF   And all my children?
ROSS   Well too.
MACDUFF   The tyrant has not battered at their peace?
ROSS   No, they were well at peace, when I did leave 'em.
MACDUFF   Be not a niggard of your speech: how goes't?   180
ROSS   When I came hither to transport the tidings
          Which I have heavily borne, there ran a rumour
          Of many worthy fellows that were out;
          Which was to my belief witnessed the rather,
          For that I saw the tyrant's power afoot.
          [*To Malcolm:*] Now is the time of help: your eye
                                            in Scotland
          Would create soldiers, make our women fight,
          To doff their dire distresses.
MALCOLM   Be't their comfort
          We are coming thither: gracious England hath
          Lent us good Seyward and ten thousand men;   190
          An older and a better soldier, none
          That Christendom gives out.
ROSS   Would I could answer
          This comfort with the like. But I have words,
          That would be howled out in the desert air,
          Where hearing should not latch them.
MACDUFF   What concern they?
          The general cause, or is it a fee-grief
          Due to some single breast?
ROSS   No mind that's honest
          But in it shares some woe, though the main part
          Pertains to you alone.
MACDUFF   If it be mine,
          Keep it not from me, quickly let me have it.   200
ROSS   Let not your ears despise my tongue for ever,
          Which shall possess them with the heaviest sound
          That ever yet they heard.
MACDUFF   H'm: I guess at it.

ROSS   Your castle is surprised; your wife and babes
               Savagely slaughtered. To relate the manner,
               Were, on the quarry of these murthered deer,
               To add the death of you.

MALCOLM   Merciful Heaven!
               [*To Macduff:*] What, man! Ne'er pull your hat upon your
                                                        brows:
               Give sorrow words: the grief that does not speak
               Whispers the o'er-fraught heart, and bids it break.   210

MACDUFF   My children too?

ROSS   Wife, children, servants, all
               That could be found.

MACDUFF   And I must be from thence!
               My wife killed too?

ROSS   I have said.

MALCOLM   Be comforted:
               Let's make us med'cines of our great revenge,
               To cure this deadly grief.

MACDUFF   [*To Ross:*] He has no children.[96] All my pretty ones?
               Did you say 'all'? O Hell-kite! All?
               What, all my pretty chickens and their dam
               At one fell swoop?

MALCOLM   Dispute it like a man.

MACDUFF   I shall do so;   220
               But I must also feel it as a man:
               I cannot but remember such things were,
               That were most precious to me. Did Heaven look on,
               And would not take their part? Sinful Macduff,
               They were all struck for thee. Naught that I am,
               Not for their own demerits, but for mine,
               Fell slaughter on their souls: Heaven rest them now!

MALCOLM   Be this the whetstone of your sword: let grief
               Convert to anger; blunt not the heart, enrage it.

MACDUFF   O, I could play the woman with mine eyes,   230
               And braggart with my tongue! But, gentle heavens,
               Cut short all intermission: front to front
               Bring thou this fiend of Scotland and myself;
               Within my sword's length set him; if he scape,
               Heaven forgive him too!

MALCOLM   This time goes manly.[97]
             Come, go we to the King; our pow'r is ready;
             Our lack is nothing but our leave. Macbeth
             Is ripe for shaking, and the pow'rs above
             Put on their instruments. Receive what cheer you may;
             The night is long that never finds the day.   240
                                              [*Exeunt*.

ACT 5, SCENE 1.

A room in Macbeth's castle at Dunsinane.

Enter a DOCTOR *of Medicine, and an* ATTENDANT-GENTLEWOMAN.

DOCTOR   I have two nights watched with you, but can perceive
                 no truth in your report. When was it she last walked?

ATTEN.   Since his Majesty went into the field, I have seen her
                 rise from her bed, throw her night-gown upon her,
                 unlock her closet, take forth paper, fold it, write
                 upon't, read it, afterwards seal it, and again return to
                 bed; yet all this while in a most fast sleep.

DOCTOR   A great perturbation in nature, to receive at once the
                 benefit of sleep and do the effects of watching. In this
                 slumbry agitation, besides her walking and other actual   10
                 performances, what (at any time) have you heard her say?

ATTEN.   That, sir, which I will not report after her.

DOCTOR   You may to me, and 'tis most meet you should.

ATTEN.   Neither to you nor anyone, having no witness to
                 confirm my speech.

                 Enter LADY MACBETH, *holding a taper.*

                 Lo you, here she comes. This is her very guise, and,
                 upon my life, fast asleep: observe her, stand close.

DOCTOR   How came she by that light?

ATTEN.   Why, it stood by her: she has light by her continually:
                 'tis her command.   [*Lady Macbeth sets the taper.*[98]   20

DOCTOR   You see, her eyes are open.

ATTEN.   Ay, but their sense are shut.

DOCTOR   What is it she does now? Look how she rubs her hands.

ATTEN.   It is an accustomed action with her, to seem thus
                 washing her hands: I have known her continue in this
                 a quarter of an hour.

LADY M.   Yet here's a spot.

DOCTOR   Hark, she speaks. I will set down what comes from
                 her, to satisfy my remembrance the more strongly.

LADY M.   Out, damned spot: out, I say! One: two: why, then 'tis   30
                 time to do't: Hell is murky. Fie, my lord, fie! A soldier,

and afeard? What need we fear who knows it, when none
can call our power to accompt? Yet who would have
thought the old man to have had so much blood in him?

DOCTOR   Do you mark that?

LADY M.   The Thane of Fife had a wife: where is she now?
What, will these hands ne'er be clean? No more o'that,
my lord, no more o'that: you mar all with this starting.

DOCTOR   Go to, go to: you have known what you should not.

ATTEN.   She has spoke what she should not, I am sure of that.   40
Heaven knows what she has known.

LADY M.   Here's the smell of the blood still: all the perfumes of
Arabia will not sweeten this little hand. Oh, oh, oh . . .

DOCTOR   What a sigh is there! The heart is sorely charged.

ATTEN.   I would not have such a heart in my bosom, for the
dignity of the whole body.

DOCTOR   Well, well, well.

ATTEN.   Pray God it be, sir.

DOCTOR   This disease is beyond my practice; yet I have known
those which have walked in their sleep who have died   50
holily in their beds.

LADY M.   Wash your hands, put on your night-gown, look not
so pale: I tell you yet again, Banquo's buried; he cannot
come out on's grave.

DOCTOR   Even so?

LADY M.   To bed, to bed; there's knocking at the gate; come,
come, come, come, give me your hand: what's done,
cannot be undone. To bed, to bed, to bed.   [Exit.

DOCTOR   Will she go now to bed?

ATTEN.   Directly.   60

DOCTOR   Foul whisp'rings are abroad: unnatural deeds
Do breed unnatural troubles: infected minds
To their deaf pillows will discharge their secrets.
More needs she the divine than the physician.
– God, God forgive us all! – Look after her,
Remove from her the means of all annoyance,
And still keep eyes upon her. So, good night.
My mind she has mated, and amazed my sight.
I think, but dare not speak.

ATTEN.   Good night, good doctor.
                                              [Exeunt.

SCENE 2.

The countryside near Dunsinane.

Enter, marching, MENTEITH, CAITHNESS, ANGUS, LENNOX, *and*
SOLDIERS *(some bearing colours) with a* DRUMMER.
Drumming ceases. They halt.

MENTEITH The English power is near, led on by Malcolm,
His uncle Seyward and the good Macduff.
Revenges burn in them, for their dear causes
Would to the bleeding and the grim alarm
Excite the mortified man.[99]

ANGUS   Near Birnam wood
Shall we well meet them: that way are they coming.

CAITHNESS Who knows if Donalbain be with his brother?

LENNOX For certain, sir, he is not: I have a file
Of all the gentry: there is Seyward's son,
And many unrough youths, that even now   10
Protest their first of manhood.

MENTEITH   What does the tyrant?

CAITHNESS Great Dunsinane he strongly fortifies.
Some say he's mad; others, that lesser hate him,
Do call it valiant fury; but, for certain,
He cannot buckle his distempered cause
Within the belt of rule.

ANGUS   Now does he feel
His secret murthers sticking on his hands;
Now minutely revolts upbraid his faith-breach;
Those he commands move only in command,
Nothing in love. Now does he feel his title   20
Hang loose about him, like a giant's robe
Upon a dwarfish thief.

MENTEITH   Who then shall blame
His pestered senses to recoil and start,
When all that is within him does condemn
Itself for being there?

CAITHNESS   Well, march we on,
To give obedience where 'tis truly owed:

Meet we the med'cine of the sickly weal,
And with him pour we, in our country's purge,
Each drop of us.[100]
LENNOX   Or so much as it needs
To dew the sovereign flower and drown the weeds.   30
Make we our march towards Birnam.
                                        [*Exeunt, marching.*

SCENE 3.

Inside Macbeth's castle at Dunsinane.

Enter MACBETH*, the* DOCTOR *and* ATTENDANTS.

MACBETH   Bring me no more reports; let them fly all:
Till Birnam Wood remove to Dunsinane,
I cannot taint with fear. What's the boy Malcolm?
Was he not born of woman? The spirits that know
All mortal consequences have pronounced me thus:
'Fear not, Macbeth; no man that's born of woman
Shall e'er have power upon thee'. Then fly, false thanes,
And mingle with the English epicures:
The mind I sway by, and the heart I bear,
Shall never sag with doubt, nor shake with fear.   10

Enter a SERVANT.

The Devil damn thee black, thou cream-faced loon!
Where got'st thou that goose look?
SERVANT   There is ten thousand –
MACBETH   Geese, villain?
SERVANT   Soldiers, sir.
MACBETH   Go prick thy face and over-red thy fear,
Thou lily-livered boy. What soldiers, patch?
Death of thy soul! Those linen cheeks of thine
Are counsellors to fear. What soldiers, whey-face?
SERVANT   The English force, so please you.
MACBETH   Take thy face hence.   [*Exit servant.*
                          Seyton! [*Aside:*] I am sick at heart,
When I behold – Seyton, I say! – This push   20
Will cheer me ever, or dis-seat me now.

I have lived long enough: my way of life
Is fall'n into the sere, the yellow leaf;
And that which should accompany old age,
As honour, love, obedience, troops of friends,
I must not look to have; but, in their stead,
Curses, not loud but deep, mouth-honour, breath
Which the poor heart would fain deny and dare not.
– Seyton!

Enter SEYTON.

SEYTON   What's your gracious pleasure?
MACBETH   What news more?   30
SEYTON   All is confirmed, my lord, which was reported.
MACBETH   I'll fight, till from my bones my flesh be hacked.
Give me my armour.
SEYTON   'Tis not needed yet.
MACBETH   I'll put it on.
Send out moe horses, skirr the country round,
Hang those that talk of fear. Give me mine armour.
                 [*Seyton goes across to fetch it.*
– How does your patient, doctor?
DOCTOR   Not so sick, my lord,
As she is troubled with thick-coming fancies
That keep her from her rest.
MACBETH   Cure her of that:
Canst thou not minister to a mind diseased,   40
Pluck from the memory a rooted sorrow,
Raze out the written troubles of the brain,
And with some sweet oblivious antidote
Cleanse the stuffed bosom of that perilous stuff
Which weighs upon the heart?
DOCTOR   Therein the patient
Must minister to himself.

Seyton returns with the armour.
An attendant prepares to equip Macbeth with it.

MACBETH   Throw physic to the dogs, I'll none of it! –
Come, put mine armour on; give me my staff. –
Seyton, send out. – Doctor, the thanes fly from me. –
Come, sir, dispatch. – If thou couldst, doctor, cast   50

The water of my land, find her disease,
And purge it to a sound and pristine health,
I would applaud thee to the very echo,
That should applaud again. – Pull't off, I say. –
What rhubarb, senna, or what purgative drug[101]
Would scour these English hence? Hear'st thou of them?

DOCTOR   Ay, my good lord; your royal preparation
            Makes us hear something.

MACBETH   – Bring it after me. –
            I will not be afraid of death and bane
            Till Birnam Forest come to Dunsinane.   60

DOCTOR   [aside:] Were I from Dunsinane away and clear,
            Profit again should hardly draw me here.   [Exeunt.

SCENE 4.

Countryside near Birnam.

Enter, marching, MALCOLM, SEYWARD, MACDUFF, SEYWARD'S SON,
MENTEITH, CAITHNESS, ANGUS, LENNOX, ROSS, *and* SOLDIERS *(some
bearing colours) with a* DRUMMER. *Drumming ceases. They halt.*

MALCOLM   Cousins, I hope the days are near at hand
            That chambers will be safe.

MENTEITH   We doubt it nothing.

SEYWARD   What wood is this before us?

MENTEITH   The Wood of Birnam.

MALCOLM   Let every soldier hew him down a bough,
            And bear't before him: thereby shall we shadow
            The numbers of our host, and make discovery
            Err in report of us.

SOLDIER   It shall be done.

SEYWARD   We learn no other but the confident tyrant
            Keeps still in Dunsinane, and will endure
            Our setting down before't.

MALCOLM   'Tis his main hope: 10
            For where there is advantage to be given,
            Both more and less have given him the revolt,[102]
            And none serve with him but constrainèd things
            Whose hearts are absent too.

MACDUFF   Let our just censures
          Attend the true event,[103] and put we on
          Industrious soldiership.
SEYWARD   The time approaches
          That will with due decision make us know
          What we shall say we have, and what we owe.
          Thoughts speculative their unsure hopes relate,
          But certain issue strokes must arbitrate: 20
          Towards which, advance the war.   [*Exeunt, marching.*

                        SCENE 5.

          Inside Macbeth's castle at Dunsinane.

     Enter MACBETH, SEYTON, *and* SOLDIERS *(some bearing colours)*
                     with a DRUMMER.

MACBETH   Hang out our banners on the outward walls.
          The cry is still 'They come'. Our castle's strength
          Will laugh a siege to scorn: here let them lie
          Till famine and the ague eat them up.
          Were they not forced with those that should be ours,
          We might have met them dareful, beard to beard,
          And beat them backward home. [*Women within cry out.*
                                      What is that noise?
SEYTON   It is the cry of women, my good lord.   [*Exit.*
MACBETH   I have almost forgot the taste of fears.
          The time has been, my senses would have cooled   10
          To hear a night-shriek, and my fell of hair
          Would at a dismal treatise rouse and stir,
          As life were in't. I have supped full with horrors;
          Direness, familiar to my slaughterous thoughts,
          Cannot once start me.
                        Enter SEYTON.

                          − Wherefore was that cry?
SEYTON   The Queen, my lord, is dead.
MACBETH   She should have died hereafter.
          There would have been a time for such a word.
          Tomorrow, and tomorrow, and tomorrow,

Creeps in this petty pace[104] from day to day,   20
To the last syllable of recorded time;
And all our yesterdays have lighted fools
The way to dusty death. Out, out, brief candle!
Life's but a walking shadow, a poor player,
That struts and frets his hour upon the stage,
And then is heard no more. It is a tale
Told by an idiot, full of sound and fury,
Signifying nothing.[105]

Enter a MESSENGER.

– Thou com'st to use thy tongue: thy story quickly.
MESSENGER Gracious my lord,   30
I should report that which I say I saw,
But know not how to do't.
MACBETH   Well, say, sir.
MESSENGER As I did stand my watch upon the hill,
I looked toward Birnam, and anon methought
The wood began to move.
MACBETH   Liar and slave!
MESSENGER Let me endure your wrath, if't be not so:
Within this three mile may you see it coming.
I say, a moving grove.
MACBETH   If thou speak'st false,
Upon the next tree shalt thou hang alive
Till famine cling thee; if thy speech be sooth,   40
I care not if thou dost for me as much.
[*Aside:*] I pull in resolution,[106] and begin
To doubt th'equivocation of the Fiend
That lies like truth. 'Fear not, till Birnam Wood
Do come to Dunsinane'; and now a wood
Comes toward Dunsinane. [*Aloud:*] Arm, arm, and out!
[*Aside:*] If this which he avouches does appear,
There is nor flying hence, nor tarrying here.
I 'gin to be aweary of the sun,
And wish th'estate o'th'world were now undone.   50
[*Aloud:*] Ring the alarum-bell! Blow wind, come wrack;
At least we'll die with harness on our back!
                                    [*Alarum. Exeunt.*

SCENE 6.

Near Macbeth's castle at Dunsinane.

Enter MALCOLM, SEYWARD, MACDUFF *and their* ARMY
(including a DRUMMER *and* TRUMPETERS).
Some soldiers bear colours; most hold boughs.

MALCOLM Now near enough: your leavy screens throw down,
And show like those you are. You, worthy uncle,
Shall with my cousin, your right noble son,
Lead our first battle. Worthy Macduff and we
Shall take upon's what else remains to do,
According to our order.

SEYWARD   Fare you well.
Do we but find the tyrant's power tonight,
Let us be beaten, if we cannot fight.

MACDUFF Make all our trumpets speak: give them all breath,
Those clamorous harbingers of blood and death!   10
                                        [*Alarums. Exeunt.*

SCENE 7.

Another part of the battlefield.

Enter MACBETH.

MACBETH They have tied me to a stake: I cannot fly,
But bear-like I must fight the course.[107] What's he
That was not born of woman? Such a one
Am I to fear, or none.

Enter YOUNG SEYWARD.

YOUNG S. What is thy name?

MACBETH   Thou'lt be afraid to hear it.

YOUNG S. No; though thou call'st thyself a hotter name
Than any is in Hell.

MACBETH   My name's Macbeth.

YOUNG S.   The Devil himself could not pronounce a title
           More hateful to mine ear.

MACBETH   No, nor more fearful.

YOUNG S.   Thou liest, abhorrèd tyrant; with my sword   10
           I'll prove the lie thou speak'st.
                       [*They fight, and young Seyward is slain.*

MACBETH   Thou wast born of woman;
           But swords I smile at, weapons laugh to scorn,
           Brandished by man that's of a woman born.   [*Exit.*

                   Alarums. Enter MACDUFF.

MACDUFF   That way the noise is. − Tyrant, show thy face!
           If thou beest slain and with no stroke of mine,
           My wife and children's ghosts will haunt me still.
           I cannot strike at wretched kerns, whose arms
           Are hired to bear their staves; either thou, Macbeth,
           Or else my sword with an unbattered edge   20
           I sheathe again undeeded. There thou shouldst be;
           By this great clatter, one of greatest note
           Seems bruited. − Let me find him, Fortune,
           And more I beg not.   [*Exit. Alarums.*

                   Enter MALCOLM *and* SEYWARD.

SEYWARD   This way, my lord; the castle's gently rendered:
           The tyrant's people on both sides do fight,
           The noble thanes do bravely in the war,
           The day almost itself professes yours,
           And little is to do.

MALCOLM   We have met with foes
           That strike beside us.

SEYWARD   Enter, sir, the castle.   30
                                   [*Exeunt. Alarum.*

SCENE 8.[108]

Another part of the battlefield.

Enter MACBETH.

MACBETH   Why should I play the Roman fool, and die
On mine own sword? Whiles I see lives, the gashes
Do better upon them.[109]

Enter MACDUFF.

MACDUFF   Turn, Hell–hound, turn!
MACBETH   Of all men else I have avoided thee;
But get thee back: my soul is too much charged
With blood of thine already.
MACDUFF   I have no words:
My voice is in my sword, thou bloodier villain
Than terms can give thee out!   [*They fight. Alarum.*
MACBETH   Thou losest labour.
As easy mayst thou the intrenchant air
With thy keen sword impress, as make me bleed.   10
Let fall thy blade on vulnerable crests:
I bear a charmèd life, which must not yield
To one of woman born.
MACDUFF   Despair thy charm,
And let the angel whom thou still hast served
Tell thee, Macduff was from his mother's womb
Untimely ripped.
MACBETH   Accursèd be that tongue that tells me so,
For it hath cowed my better part of man;[110]
And be these juggling fiends no more believed,
That palter with us in a double sense,   20
That keep the word of promise to our ear,
And break it to our hope. I'll not fight with thee.
MACDUFF   Then yield thee, coward,
And live to be the show and gaze o'th'time.
We'll have thee, as our rarer monsters are,
Painted upon a pole, and underwrit,
'Here may you see the tyrant'.[111]
MACBETH   I will not yield,

To kiss the ground before young Malcolm's feet,
And to be baited with the rabble's curse.
Though Birnam Wood be come to Dunsinane,   30
And thou opposed, being of no woman born,
Yet I will try the last. Before my body
I throw my warlike shield. Lay on, Macduff,
And damned be him that first cries 'Hold, enough'!
      [*Exeunt fighting. Alarum. Enter fighting. Macbeth is slain.*
                        Exit Macduff with Macbeth's body.

SCENE 9.

Within the castle.

Retreat and flourish. Enter MALCOLM, SEYWARD, ROSS, THANES,
and SOLDIERS *(some bearing colours) with a* DRUMMER.

MALCOLM I would the friends we miss were safe arrived.
SEYWARD Some must go off; and yet, by these I see,
So great a day as this is cheaply bought.
MALCOLM Macduff is missing, and your noble son.
ROSS [*to Seyward:*] Your son, my lord, has paid a soldier's debt:
He only lived but till he was a man,
The which no sooner had his prowess confirmed
In the unshrinking station where he fought,
But like a man he died.
SEYWARD   Then he is dead?
ROSS Ay, and brought off the field. Your cause of sorrow   10
Must not be measured by his worth, for then
It hath no end.
SEYWARD   Had he his hurts before?
ROSS Ay, on the front.
SEYWARD   Why then, God's soldier be he!
Had I as many sons as I have hairs,
I would not wish them to a fairer death:
And so his knell is knolled.
MALCOLM   He's worth more sorrow,
And that I'll spend for him.

SEYWARD   He's worth no more.
They say he parted well, and paid his score,
And so God be with him. Here comes newer comfort.

Enter MACDUFF, *bearing Macbeth's head on a pole.*[112]

MACDUFF [*To Malcolm:*] Hail, King, for so thou art. Behold,
                                   where stands   20
Th'usurper's cursèd head: the time is free.
I see thee compassed with thy kingdom's pearl,[113]
That speak my salutation in their minds;
Whose voices I desire aloud with mine:
Hail, King of Scotland!

ALL   Hail, King of Scotland! [*Flourish.*

MALCOLM We shall not spend a large expense of time
Before we reckon with your several loves,
And make us even with you. My thanes and kinsmen,
Henceforth be earls, the first that ever Scotland
In such an honour named. What's more to do,   30
Which would be planted newly with the time,
As calling home our exiled friends abroad
That fled the snares of watchful tyranny,
Producing forth the cruel ministers
Of this dead butcher and his fiend-like Queen,
(Who, as 'tis thought, by self and violent hands
Took off her life): this, and what needful else
That calls upon us, by the grace of Grace
We will perform in measure, time, and place.
So thanks to all at once, and to each one,   40
Whom we invite to see us crowned at Scone.
                               [*Flourish. Exeunt omnes.*

FINIS.

NOTES ON *MACBETH*

In these notes, the following abbreviations are used:

Bullough: *Narrative and Dramatic Sources of Shakespeare*, Vol. VII, ed. Geoffrey Bullough (London: Routledge & Kegan Paul, 1973).

cf.: *confer* (Latin): compare.

Dæmonologie: James VI of Scotland (James I of England): *Dæmonologie* (1597; rpt., London: Bodley Head, 1924).

e.g.: *exempli gratia* (Latin): for example.

F1: The First Folio (1623).

F2: The Second Folio (1632).

Holinshed: Raphael Holinshed and others: *The Chronicles of England, Scotland, and Ireland*, Vol. II (1587); as selected in Bullough.

i.e.: *id est* (Latin): that is; in other words.

O.E.D.: *The Oxford English Dictionary* (website).

Scot: Reginald Scot: *A Discoverie of Witchcraft* (1584; rpt., New York: Dover, 1972).

S.D.: stage-direction.

Unless otherwise indicated, Biblical quotations are from the Geneva Bible (1560), though I modernise its spelling and punctuation.

Where a pun, a metaphor or an ambiguity is glossed, the meanings are distinguished as (a) and (b), or (a), (b) and (c); otherwise, different meanings are distinguished as (i) and (ii), etc.

1 (title) *MACBETH*: In the First Folio (F1), the opening title is '*The Tragedie of Macbeth*'.

2 (1.1, S.D.) *WITCHES*.: Although the F1 stage-directions use the term 'witches', the F1 dialogue usually refers to them as the 'weyward Sisters' or 'weyard Sisters'. Both adjectives connote 'wayward', 'strange, perverse and unnatural', 'weird' and (thereby) 'fateful', thus invoking a wider range of meaning (while fitting the metre better) than 'weird' alone.

3 (1.1.8) *Gray-Malkin . . . Anon!*: 'Gray-Malkin' meant 'Little Grey Mall [*or* Moll]', a name used for a cat; 'Padock' (often 'Paddock') meant 'Toad'. Both cats and toads were deemed witches' familiars (evil helpers). 'Anon' meant 'at once' or 'very soon'. F1 attributes to '*All*' witches its words after '*Gray-Malkin.*'.

4 (1.2, S.D.) Alarum . . . CAPTAIN.: '*Alarum*' could mean (a) 'a summons (by trumpet, bell or other means) of troops to battle', (b) 'sounds of battle', or (c) both these. '*Within*' means '*offstage*'. A 'captain' could also be a sergeant, as the dialogue shows. The F1 spelling, 'Serieant', may indicate trisyllabic pronunciation.

5 (1.2.14–20) *And Fortune . . . slave;*: In lines 14–15, 'Fortune' (deity of changing luck and chance) is like a 'rebel's whore' because she smiles on this rebel at first, giving him initial success, but later abandons him. Here 'quarrel' is an editorial emendation of F1's 'Quarry'. Line 18 has regular pentameter if the 'ion' of 'execution' is pronounced as two syllables; similarly, in line 19, the 'ion' of 'minion' can be disyllabic.

6 (1.2.25–8) *As whence . . . swells.* Possibly: 'When, at the vernal equinox, the sun begins his return to full strength, there arise from that direction woeful thunder and storms which wreck ships; similarly, from the area from which relief seemed to come, trouble grows.' Alternatively: 'From the east, where the sun rises, dangerous thunder and shipwrecking storms come; similarly [etc.].'

7 (1.2.51) *Norway . . . terrible,*: In F1, the line ends with 'terrible numbers'. To restore the metre, I invert the order of those two words, producing what was probably intended originally: cf. 'accents terrible' in 2.3.54.

8 (1.2.54–5) *Till . . . self-comparisons,*: 'until Macbeth, like the bride-groom of Bellona (the Roman war-goddess), clad in strongest armour, confronted him with qualities that matched his own,'.

9 (1.2.62) *Saint Colmè's Inch,*: (F1 has 'Saint *Colmes* ynch,'.) 'Inch' is Gaelic for 'Island'. 'Saint Colmè' is St. Columba. The island was later called 'Inchcomb'. I accentuate 'Colmè' as disyllabic but iambic ('*Cól*-mè').

10 (1.3.8–26) *Her . . . tempest-tossed.*: In 1625, Samuel Purchas reported that a real vessel called *Tiger* (or *Tigre*) had endured an arduous voyage from 5 December 1604 to 9 July 1606: approximately 'nine times nine' weeks. In line 12, 'wind' rhymes with 'kind', its long 'i' being normal until the 19th century. Lines 17–18 mean 'all the four main directions that they know in the mariner's compass-card.'.

11 (1.3.47–8) *And yet . . . so.*: Some witches were said to be bearded.

12 (1.3.72) *By . . . death,*: 'By the death of Sinell, my father,'. Historically, the name began with 'F' (its spellings including 'Finel' and 'Findlaech'), but chroniclers such as Holinshed mis-spelt it. (At line 40, F1 rendered Holinshed's 'Forres' as 'Soris'.)

13 (1.3, S.D. after 79) *[The . . . vanish.*: F1 has '*Witches vanish*'. In the theatre, perhaps a trap-door and smoke were used.

14 (1.3.85–6) *the insane . . . prisoner?*: The 'insane root' (root causing insanity when eaten) may be hemlock, henbane or belladonna.

15 (1.3.96–9) *He finds . . . post,*: 'He learns that you were in the thick of the battle against the ranks of stalwart Norwegians, having no fear of those whom you made into foreign representations of death [i.e. whom you slew]. The speedy messengers arrived as densely as hail,'.

16 (1.3.112–15) *Which . . . not;*: In F1, this passage's lines end with 'loose.' (i.e. 'lose.'), 'Norway,', 'helpe,', 'labour'd' and 'not:'. As at other places in the text, editors variously emend the arrangement of lines in the hope of improving the metre.

17 (1.3.121–3) *That . . . Cawdor.*: 'That prophecy, fully trusted, might henceforth incite you to become King Macbeth after becoming the Thane of Cawdor.'

18 (1.3.140) *My . . . fantastical,*: 'my thinking, whose conception of murder is as yet only fanciful,'.

19 (1.3.147–8) *Come . . . day.*: 'Whatever may befall, and however turbulent the events, time proceeds steadily.' (This may imply: 'Let time decide; I'll wait and see.')

20 (1.3.151–3) *your . . . them.*: 'your endeavours are recorded in the book of my memory, and every day I will turn the page to read that record.': i.e. 'I'll never forget your help.'

21 (1.4.27) *Safe . . . honour.*: 'to safeguard your loving and honourable self.'

22 (1.4.34–5) *Wanton . . . sorrow.*: 'recklessly ample, seek to disguise themselves in tears (usually the sign of sorrow).'

23 (1.5.21–4) *Thou'dst . . . undone.*: 'Lord Glamis, to gain what you seek, you need it to shout "This is what you must do!"; and you desire what you fear doing but wouldn't wish to leave not done.'

24 (1.5.37–9) *The raven . . . battlements.*: The raven's cry was supposed to portend death. Line 38 can be regularised by stretching 'entrance' as 'enterance' (as 56 can be aided by pronouncing 'feel' disyllabically); cf. 'remembrance' at 3.2.35. A pause before 'Come' mends the metre of line 39.

25 (1.5.39–49) *Come . . . mischief.*: Here, 'mortal thoughts' are both (a) deadly thoughts and (b) human thoughts; 'unsex me' means 'remove my womanly nature'; and 'compunctious visitings of nature' are 'considerate accesses of natural feelings'. 'And take my milk for gall' means 'and for my maternal milk substitute bitter bile', while 'sightless substances' are 'invisible presences' (of evil spirits).

26 (1.5.70–71) *Only . . . fear.*: 'Simply look on innocently and serenely: to deviate in your appearance means constant anxiety [*or* is always to be feared].'

27 (1.6.4–8) *The temple-haunting . . . cradle:*: The 'martlet' ('Barlet' in F1) is the swift or the house-martin; 'mansionry' means 'house-building'; 'jutty', 'frieze', 'coign of vantage' and 'procreant' mean (respectively) 'overhanging part', 'area between the lintel and the cornice above it', 'convenient corner' and 'for offspring'.

28 (1.6.11–14) *The love . . . trouble.*: 'The loving attention conferred on us is sometimes a nuisance, but we still offer thanks as if it were only loving attention. By saying this, I teach you how to ask God to thank us for your work, while you thank us for being a nuisance to you.'

29 (1.7.6–7) *But . . . come.*: 'just here, on this temporal sandbank or shallow, we would evade the afterlife [and consequently the possibility of punishment in Hell].'. F1 has 'Banke and Schoole' (which can mean 'bench and school', anticipating the later references to teaching) where most editors prefer to read 'bank and shoal'.

30 (1.7.22–3) *Heaven's . . . air,*: 'heavenly angels, riding like horse-borne messengers the invisible [*or* blind] winds,'.

31 (1.7.44–5) *Letting . . . i'th'adage?*: The adage (which has variants) is: 'The cat wanted to eat fish but dared not get her feet wet.'

32 (1.7.47) *Who . . . none.*: 'the person who dares to do more than befits a man is not really a man [for he's madly presumptuous].' To fit the context, editors often emend as 'do more' F1's 'no more'.

33 (1.7.58–9) *had . . . this.*: (a) 'if, like you, I had sworn to do this and then flinched from doing it.'; (b:) 'if I had made your murderous resolution.'.

34 (1.7.60) *screw . . . sticking-place,*: (a) 'brace your courage, like someone winding the string of a crossbow to the point where it is held taut until triggered,'; or (b) ' . . . someone tightening a screw until it can move no more,'; or (c) ' . . . someone tightening the string of an instrument until it is taut,'.

35 (2.1, S.D.) Enter . . . BANQUO.: F1 has '*Enter Banquo, and Fleance, with a Torch before him.*' I put Fleance first, as the torch-bearer normally leads, lighting the way for the other (and more important) person. Cf. the S.D. after line 10.

36 (2.1.18–20) *Being . . . wrought.*: 'As we were not prepared for his arrival, our wish to be hospitable was hampered by shortages; otherwise we could have been freely generous.'

37 (2.1.45–6) *Mine . . . rest:*: 'Either my eyes are fools, mocked by the fact that my other senses register no dagger, or else they are so perceptive that they are equal in value to all the other senses put together:'.

38 (2.1.50–57) *Now . . . earth,*: The 'one half-world' is the earth's hemisphere which is now in darkness. Sleep is 'curtained' by either bed-curtains or eyelids. In ceremonies by witches, sacrificial offerings may be made to Heccat, the goddess of witchcraft. Heccat (whose name, outside the play, is often spelt 'Hecate') is 'pale' because she is also the moon-goddess. Shakespeare's narrative poem, *The Rape of Lucrece*, had retold the legend of the nocturnal rape by Tarquin, King of Rome, of the chaste Lucrece (Lucretia), who subsequently committed suicide. Tarquin was later slain in revenge. (In lines 56 and 57, 'strides' and 'sure' emend F1's 'sides' and 'sowre'.)

39 (2.1.60) *And take . . . time,*: 'and remove the horrifying stillness which prevails at present,'.

40 (2.2.3–4) *the owl . . . good-night.*: A 'bellman' is a night-watchman. The owl's cry was regarded as ill-omened, a portent of death.

41 (2.2.27) *hangman's hands.*: A hangman's duties sometimes included drawing (disembowelling) and quartering the victim, so his hands would become amply bloodstained; and he could also be employed to chop off a head with an axe.

42 (2.2.37–9) *ravelled . . . course,*: 'ravelled sleeve': either (a) frayed sleeve of a garment, or (b) tangled silk. The phrase 'second course' likens sleep to the second part of a meal, the waking-state being the first part.

43 (2.2.56–7) *gild . . . guilt.*: grim punning. (Some gold was reddish in hue. Sometimes blood was termed 'golden' and gold was termed 'red'.)

44 (2.2.63) *Making the green one red.*: (a) 'making red the "green one" (the ocean).'; (b) 'making the green ocean "one red"', one expanse of redness.'.

45 (2.2.67–9) *A little . . . unattended.*: On the 'little water', cf.. Act 5,
Scene 1, and Pilate in Matthew 27:24. Her last sentence means:
'Your firmness of purpose has deserted you.'

46 (2.2.73) *To know . . . myself.*: 'If I am to acknowledge my crime, I
must change my nature.'

47 (2.3.1–20) *Here's . . . porter.*: The porter, still inebriated, imagines
himself to be the door-keeper of Hell. In line 2, 'old' means
'ample'. 'Belzebub' (line 3–4) is 'Beelzebub', which, according to
Matthew 12:24, is another name of Satan, but, according to
Marlowe and other writers, is the name of a different devil. The
farmer 'that hanged himself ' is usually regarded by editors as one
who hoarded grain to profit from dearth but was financially ruined
when the harvest proved abundant. The 'equivocator' lines perhaps
allude to Father Garnet, a Jesuit (hanged for his involvement in the
Gunpowder Plot of 1605) who had argued that persecuted Catholics
were entitled to equivocate during interrogation. The tailor was
presumably keeping for himself some of the material that he was
supposed to make into French-style breeches. In the fires of Hell he
can 'roast [his] goose', meaning: (a) 'have his goose cooked' (be
vanquished); and (b) 'heat his smoothing-iron'.

48 (2.3.22) *the second cock;*: 3 a.m., according to *Romeo and Juliet*, Act
4, Scene 4.

49 (2.3.31–2) *stand . . . him.*: Here 'stand to, and not stand to' means
'gain and lose an erection'; 'equivocates him in a sleep' means (a)
'tricks him into falling asleep' and (b) 'tricks him in his dreams'; and
'giving him the lie' means (a) 'declaring him a liar', (b) 'making
him lie down', and (c) 'making him urinate' (since 'Lye', F1's
spelling here, could mean 'urine').

50 (2.3.36–7) *though . . . him.*: (a) 'though, like a wrestler, he sometimes heaved my legs to make me fall, I made a good attempt to
throw him off.'; (b) 'though he sometimes made me feel legless, I
did my best to vomit him out.'.

51 (2.3.56) *The óbscure bird*: the bird of darkness: the ominous owl,
which hunts at night.

52 (2.3.65) *The Lord's anointed temple*: 'the sacred body of the king'.
The Bible (e.g. in 1 Corinthians 3:16 and 1 Samuel 24:10) declares
that man is 'the temple of God' and that a king (specifically Saul) is
'the Lord's anointed'. In a coronation ceremony, a monarch
would be anointed as part of his or her installation as God's deputy
on earth.

53 (2.3.75) *The great doom's image!*: 'an image of Doomsday (when all the dead will present themselves for judgement)!'

54 (2.3.118–19) *where . . . us?*: Scot (p. 6) reports the belief that witches 'can go in and out at awger holes'. An auger is a carpenter's piercing-tool.

55 (2.3.121) *Nor . . . motion.*: 'And our powerful grief has not yet started to express itself.'

56 (2.3.123–4) *when . . . exposure,*: (a) 'when we have concealed our exposed weaknesses (tears of grief),'; (b) 'when we have properly covered our exposed bodies,'.

57 (2.3.137–8) *the near . . . bloody.*: 'those who are close in blood-relationship (to the dead king) are closest to a bloody destiny.'

58 (2.3.142–3) *there's warrant . . . left.*: 'stealing is justified when it's a matter of stealing away from a merciless occasion.'

59 (2.4.30) *The sovereignty . . . Macbeth.*: The Scottish monarchy was sometimes elective and sometimes hereditary. Duncan's sons have fled, and Macbeth is his first cousin and a successful warrior. (Subsequently in the play, Macbeth is King of Scotland and his wife is Queen; but F1's speech-prefixes continue to call them '*Macb.*' and '*Lady*', and editors customarily follow F1 in not changing their speech-prefixes.)

60 (2.4.31, 33) *Scone . . . Colmekill,*: Scone, an abbey north of Perth, held the 'Stone of Destiny', on which Scottish kings were crowned. Colmekill, i.e. Iona, a Hebridean island, was the burial-place of Scottish kings and the location of the monastery of St. Columba.

61 (3.1.22) *we'll take tomorrow.*: 'we will use part of tomorrow for the purpose of hearing your advice.' Macbeth uses the royal plural. (Some editors emend F1's 'take' as 'take't' or 'talk'.)

62 (3.1.54–6) *under . . . Cæsar.*: Plutarch, the classical biographer, reported the notion that Mark Antony's 'Genius' (guardian spirit) was defeated by Octavius Cæsar's, and Shakespeare uses the report in *Antony and Cleopatra*, Act 2, Scene 3.

63 (3.1.67–8) *mine . . . man,*: 'given my soul, which should be like an everlasting jewel, to Satan, the enemy of all people,'.

64 (3.1.70–71) *come . . . th'utterance.*: 'let Fate enter the tournament-ground and challenge me to the uttermost.' ('Champion' could mean either 'support' or 'challenge', and the latter meaning fits better here.)

65 (3.1.129) *Acquaint . . . time,*: Editors offer divergent interpretations. Perhaps it means: 'and I will give you the most precise
estimate of the best time'. Dr Johnson thought that the 'perfect
spy' was the third murderer, who appears in Scene 3.

66 (3.2.18–19) *let . . . suffer,*: 'let the structure of all things fall apart
and both this world and the next suffer,'.

67 (3.2.46–9) *ere . . . note.*: 'before, in response to the call of black-
clad Heccat, the sleepily-humming beetle (borne on scaly wings)
has acted as the bellman whose toll says it's nightfall and yawn-
time, there will be effected a deed of a dreadful nature [*or* a deed to
become notoriously dreadful].' Shards are elytra, the beetle's wing-
cases, or, loosely, scaly wings. Some editors prefer 'shard-born'
(born from dung) to 'shard-borne' (F1's spelling); but the context
indicates flight.

68 (3.2.54–6) *that . . . wood::* 'that great bond' may be: (a) the bond of
moral obligations; (b) Banquo's lease of life. Some editors emend
F1's 'pale' as 'paled': i.e. 'fenced in', 'confined'. 'Light thickens'
means partly 'Twilight grows', but there is a more sinister con-
notation: *Dæmonologie* (p. 39) speculates that the Devil may, to
render witches invisible, 'thicken & obscure so the air'.

69 (3.3.2–4) *He . . . just.*: 'We need not mistrust this third agent,
since he specifies our duties and our tasks exactly as we were
directed to expect.'

70 (3.4.14) *'Tis . . . within.*: 'It's better outside you than inside him.'

71 (3.4.33–7) *The feast . . . without it.*: 'Unless, while a feast is
proceeding, there are frequent assurances that it is freely bestowed,
it is no better than a meal that is sold [e.g. by an innkeeper]. If you
merely need nourishment, you should stay at home; if you dine
away from there, ceremonial hospitality is the sauce that makes the
food delicious, and social gatherings would be bleak without it.'

72 (3.4.72–3) *our monuments . . . kites.*: (a) 'the craws of kites (rap-
acious birds) will eventually serve as tombs.'; (b) 'we must let kites'
craws serve as our tombs, to make sure we don't return from the
dead.' (Cf. Scot, p. 58.)

73 (3.4.77) *Ere . . . weal;*: 'before human [*or* humane] laws tamed the
commonwealth and made it civilised'. (F1 has the ambiguous
adjective 'humane', which could mean 'human'.)

74 (3.4.106–7) *If . . . girl.*: The first part can mean either (a) 'if I
exhibit trembling then', or (b) 'if, trembling, I then stay indoors'.
'The baby of a girl' means (a) 'a baby girl', or (b) 'a girl's doll'.

75 (3.4.123–7) *It will . . . blood.*: 'Blood will have blood' was already proverbial, and some associations here are biblical. In Genesis 9:6, God says: 'Whoso sheddeth man's blood, by man shall his blood be shed.'; and, in Genesis 4:10, God tells Cain: 'The voice of thy brother's blood cryeth unto me from the ground.'. The stone sealing the sepulchre of Jesus moved aside (Luke 24:2), and Jesus walked the earth after his apparent death. *Henry VI, Part 2*, Act 1, Scene 4, says that at midnight 'ghosts break up their graves'. Scot (p. 94), describing fraudulent oracles devised by priests, says: 'This practise began in the okes of Dodona, in the which was a wood, the trees thereof (they saie) could speake.' In addition, Scot (p. 119) reports the claim that 'trees spake . . . before the death of *Cæsar*'. 'Augures and understood relations' are auguries and deciphered connections. '[M]aggot-pies and choughs' are magpies and small crows. Macbeth recalls that birds have helped diviners to identify even the best-hidden murderers. Crows (e.g. magpies, choughs and rooks) are birds of ill-omen, associated with death.

76 (3.4.143–4) *My . . . use::* 'My alien and private affliction [*or* personal aberration – seeing a ghost] expresses a novice's fear; I need to be hardened by practice:'. 'Self ' could mean 'personal, private', as in 5.9.36's 'self and violent hands'.

77 (3.5, S.D. after 33:) Music . . . away'.: F1 has the S.D. '*Musicke, and a Song.*'. There the song is unspecified, but the music probably initiates the song indicated in F1's S.D. two lines later: '*Song within. Come away, come away, &c.*'. (There, '*within*' appears to mean '*from a gallery overlooking the stage*'.) Heccat's two lines at 34–5 apparently respond to the song's opening words. Although F1 states only the first line of the lyric, a full text is printed in Thomas Middleton's play *The Witch* (*c.* 1610), Act 3, Scene 3. What follows below is based on that text and its accompanying stage business. I modernise and revise the version given in the Malone Society reprint of *The Witch* (Oxford: Oxford U. P., 1963, pp. 57–9).

SPIRITS ABOVE	Come away, come away,
	Heccat, Heccat, come away.
HECCAT	I come, I come, I come, I come,
	With all the speed I may,
	With all the speed I may.
	Where's Stadlin?
SPIRIT ABOVE	Here.

HECCAT	Where's Puckle?
ANOTHER SPIRIT	Here.
SPIRITS ABOVE	And Hoppo, too, and Hellwain, too,

We lack but you, we lack but you.
Come away, make up the count.

HECCAT   I will but 'noint, and then I mount.

[MALKIN, *a spirit like a cat, descends.*]

SPIRITS ABOVE There's one comes down to fetch his dues,
A kiss, a coll, a sip of blood;
And why thou stay'st so long I muse, I muse,
Since the air's so sweet and good.

HECCAT   O, art thou come? What news, what news?

MALKIN   All goes still to our delight.
Either come, or else refuse, refuse.

HECCAT   Now I am furnished for the flight.

FIRESTONE Hark, hark: the cat sings a brave treble in her
own language.

HECCAT [*going up with Malkin:*]
Now I go, now I fly,
Malkin (my sweet spirit) and I.
Oh, what a dainty pleasure 'tis,
To ride in the air
When the moon shines fair,
And sing, and dance, and toy, and kiss.
Over woods, high rocks and mountains,
Over seas, our mistress' fountains,
Over steep towers and turrets,
We fly by night, 'mongst troops of spirits.
No ring of bells to our ears sounds,
No howls of wolves, no yelps of hounds.
No, not the noise of waters'-breach
Or cannons' throat our height can reach.

SPIRITS ABOVE No ring of bells to our ears sounds,
No howls of wolves, no yelps of hounds.
No, not the noise of waters'-breach
Or cannons' throat our height can reach.

The line 'Over seas, our mistress' fountains' is evidently corrupt:
Davenant's text of 1674 reads 'Over Hills, and misty Fountains';
and Davenant renders the next line as 'Over Steeples, Towers, and
Turrets', restoring the metre.

78 (3.6.24–9) *The son . . . respect*.: The opening means: 'Malcolm, the
elder son of Duncan (from whom this tyrant, Macbeth, withholds
his birthright)'. The 'most pious Edward' is Edward the Confessor,
King of England from 1042 to 1066, and the last of the royal Saxon
line. He was canonised in 1161.

79 (3.6.40–41) *and with . . . back,*: 'and, on receiving Macduff's absolute
refusal to join Macbeth ("Sir, not I"), the frowning messenger
turned his back,'.

80 (4.1, S.D. after 43) Music . . . spirits', etc.: This song appears in
Middleton's *The Witch*, Act 5, Scene 2. I give it below, again
emending the text of the Malone Society reprint (pp. 87–8).

A Charm Song: about a Vessel.

HECCAT	Black spirits and white, red spirits and grey,
	Mingle, mingle, mingle, you that mingle may.
	Titty, Tiffin:
	Keep it stiff in;
	Firedrake, Puckey:
	Make it lucky;
	Liand, Robin:
	You must bob in.
	Round, around, around, about, about:
	All ill come running in, all good keep out!
WITCH 4	Here's the blood of a bat.
HECCAT	Put in that, O put in that!
WITCH 5	Here's leopard's bane.
HECCAT	Put in again.
WITCH 6	The juice of toad, the oil of adder.
WITCH 4	Those will make the younker madder.
HECCAT	Put in: there's all; and rid the stench.
WITCH 5	Nay, here's three ounces of the red-haired wench.
ALL	Round, around, around, about, about:
	All ill come running in, all good keep out!

81 (4.1, S.D. after 68) *FIRST . . . sight.*: F1 has: '1. *Apparition, an Armed
Head.*' The helmeted head may be Macbeth's (which will be cut off
later), Macduff's, or Macdonald's: editors are uncertain. (Macbeth
does not identify the apparition.) It could simply be an unspecific
martial apparition portending Macbeth's death in combat with
Macduff.

82 (4.1, S.D. after 76) SECOND... sight.: F1 has: '2 *Apparition, a Bloody Childe*.' Editors have suggested that this apparition may represent: the baby Macduff, born by Cæsarean section; or Fleance; or Macduff 's murdered son. Again, it may be simply an ironic image to mislead Macbeth while portending the Cæsarean irony.

83 (4.1, S.D. at 86) THIRD... sight.: F1 has '3 *Apparition, a Childe Crowned, with a Tree in his hand*.' This is another ironic image. While the apparition purports to reassure Macbeth, it portends the 'mobile wood' stratagem, and reminds us that a child (Banquo's Fleance) will live on to engender the Stuart line or 'family tree'.

84 (4.1.112–24) *Thou ... so?*: Banquo's Ghost smiles because the Stuart monarchs are his descendants. James VI, the eighth Stuart king of Scotland, became James I of England, uniting the two realms. Scottish kings were invested with one orb and one sceptre, English kings with one orb and two sceptres.

85 (4.1.145–6) *The flighty ... with it.*: 'the fleeting intention can never be fulfilled unless action is immediate.'

86 (4.2.22) *Each ... move.*: This phrase follows F1. The meaning can be: 'following every direction and movement.'. Some editors emend 'move' as 'none', yielding: 'following all and no directions.'.

87 (4.2.34–6) *Poor ... for.*: 'Poor [i.e. unfortunate] bird! You would never fear the devices set to catch you: the net, the gluey lime, the covered pit, the spring-trap.' 'Why should I, mother? Such devices are not set for poor [i.e. worthless] birds.'

88 (4.2.64) *in ... perfect.*: 'I am fully aware of your honourable status.'

89 (4.3.14–15) *something ... me,*: 'you may discern in me some characteristics of Macbeth,'. Some editors emend F1's 'discerne' as 'deserve'.

90 (4.3.22) *though ... fell.*: Lucifer ('Lightbearer'), brightest of the angels, fell from Heaven to Hell, according to a tradition linked to Isaiah 14:12–15.

91 (4.3.29–30) *Let ... safeties::* 'do not regard my suspicions as insults to you; they stem from my concern for my safety:'.

92 (4.3.34) *The title is affeared.*: (a) 'The true claimant to the throne is frightened away.'; (b) 'What I've called "tyranny" is confirmed.' The former version is more likely: cf. 'untitled tyrant' in line 104. The latter version reads 'affeared' as 'affeered'.

93 (4.3.111) *Died ... lived.*: 'made every day a preparation for the afterlife by virtuously mortifying herself.'

94 (4.3.136–7) *the chance . . . quarrel!*: 'may our good luck be proportionate to the justice of our cause!'

95 (4.3.142–5) *their . . . amend.*: 'their disease vanquishes the great endeavours of medical skill; but, at the King's touch, they are promptly healed (for Heaven has granted such holiness to his hand).' From the time of Edward the Confessor until the reign of Queen Anne, English monarchs ceremonially touched people who suffered from scrofula (known as 'The King's Evil').

96 (4.3.216) *He . . . children.*: I assume that Macduff addresses Ross and means: 'If Malcolm had children, he would know that my grief is too great to be thus cured.' (Less likely interpretations are that Macduff addresses Malcolm and means either 'Macbeth has no children, so the revenge will not be proportionate.', or 'If Macbeth had children, he would not have slaughtered mine.'.)

97 (4.3.235) *This . . . manly.*: I follow F1, the meaning then being: 'This is the time for bold action.' Some editors emend 'time' as 'tune', to produce: 'Now you are uttering manly music.'

98 (5.1, S.D. at 20) *[Lady . . . taper.*: I supply this S.D. so that, having put down or fixed the taper, Lady Macbeth can mime hand-washing.

99 (5.2.4–5) *Would . . . man.*: 'would urge even a dead or dying man to answer the grim summons to battle and bloodshed.'

100 (5.2.29) *Each . . . us.*: (a) 'each of us as a drop of purgative medicine.'; (b) 'each drop of blood that we shed to serve as the purgative.'

101 (5.3.55) *What . . . drug*: This rhubarb is an oriental rootstock, imported for medicinal use as a purgative. Here 'senna' (the name of a laxative) is the emendation by the Fourth Folio (1685) of F1's 'Cyme', which was perhaps a misreading of 'cynne' (meaning 'senna').

102 (5.4.11–12) *where . . . revolt,*: 'where Macbeth could have gained an advantage from their loyalty, both greater and lesser people have revolted against him,'. In line 11, some editors emend F1's 'giuen' ('given') as 'gone'.

103 (5.4.14–15) *Let . . . event,*: 'Let us await the final outcome before pronouncing judicious condemnation,'.

104 (5.5.20) *Creeps . . . pace*: If 'pace' is the subject of the verb, the sense is: 'this paltry progression creeps along'. If 'Tomorrow, and tomorrow, and tomorrow,' is the subject, the sense is:

'creeps, in this slow progress,' or 'creeps, in this narrow passage,'.

105 (5.5.22–8) *And all . . . nothing.*: Job 8:9 states: '[We] are but of yesterday, and know nothing, because our days on earth are a shadow.' Echoing Genesis 3:19, 'dust thou art, and unto dust shalt thou return', the Anglican 'Order for the Burial of the Dead' says: 'Man . . . fleeth as it were a shadow; . . . ashes to ashes, dust to dust'. Lucian's *Necromantia* compares life to a play in which different actors wear diverse costumes. A proverbial saying is: 'This world is a stage and every man plays his part.': cf. Jaques' speech beginning 'All the world's a stage' in *As You Like It*, Act 2, Scene 7. Psalm 90:9 (Bishops' Bible, 1584,) includes: '[W]e bring our years to an end, as it were a tale that is told.'

106 (5.5.42) *I pull . . . resolution,*: 'I curb my resolve,'. F1 has 'pull'; some editors emend it as 'pall'.

107 (5.7.1–2) *They . . . course.*: Macbeth likens himself to a bear, which, in the cruel sport of bear-baiting, was tied to a stake and attacked by dogs.

108 (5.8, heading) SCENE 8.: F1 lets Scene 7 extend to the end of the play. Most editors let Scenes 8 and 9 be specified (as in this edition) at two of the several points at which the stage is temporarily devoid of players.

109 (5.8.1–3) *Why . . . them.*: Ancient Roman warriors (e.g. Brutus and Antony) deemed suicide nobler than surrender.

110 (5.8.18) *cowed . . . man;*: 'intimidated my manly spirit;'.

111 (5.8.26–7) *Painted . . . tyrant'.*: 'painted on a board supported by a pole, and inscribed beneath it the words "Here you may see the tyrant".' (He recalls shows in fair-grounds.)

112 (5.9, S.D. after 19) *on a pole.*: F1 does not specify the pole, but Holinshed (p. 505) does, and lines 20–21 show that the head is aloft.

113 (5.9.22) *I . . . pearl,*: 'I see you surrounded by the finest men of the realm,'. (Pearls may encircle a royal crown, adorning its rim.)

GLOSSARY

Where a pun, a metaphor or an ambiguity occurs, the meanings are distinguished as (a) and (b), or (a), (b) and (c), etc. Otherwise, alternative meanings are distinguished as (i) and (ii), or as (i), (ii) and (iii), etc. Abbreviations include the following: adj., adjective; adv., adverb; astrol., astrological; e.g., for example; fig., figuratively; Fr., French; interj., interjection; lit., literally; n., noun; *O.E.D.*, *Oxford English Dictionary*; S.D., stage-direction; vb., verb.

absolute: positive.

Acheron: dark river of the underworld; **Pit of Acheron**: entrance to Hades.

accurs'd, accurst: cursed.

actual: active.

addition: title.

addressed: prepared.

adhere: cohere; agree.

admired: amazing; surprising.

afeard: afraid.

affeared: 4.3.34: (a) scared off; (b) affeered: confirmed.

affection: desire.

agitation: activity; **slumbry agitation**: sleep-walking.

alarm: 5.2.4: onslaught.

alarum (n.): as at 1.2, S.D.: (a) summons (by trumpet, bell or other means) to battle; (b) noise of battle; (c) both; **alarum-bell**: tocsin: bell of warning.

alarum (vb.): call to action.

Aleppo (Halab): Syrian city.

All hail: 1.3.49, 50, 51: (a) All good health to; (b) Full salutation to; **all-hail** (noun): salutation (for a king); **all-hail** (vb.): greet as; salute.

all-thing: altogether.

altogether: 4.1.59: (a) all together; (b) utterly.

amazed: 2.3.105; 5.1.68: (a) bewildered; (b) astounded; **amazèdly**: distractedly; **amazement**: stupefaction.

and't: if it.

anon: at once; very soon.

annoyance: harm.

antic: quaint; fantastic.

anticipate: forestall.

approve: prove.

argument: topic; theme.

aroynt thee: be gone.

art: 1.4.11; 4.3.143: special skill.

artificial: made by special skill (e.g. magic).

assay: endeavour.

audit: **make their audit**: submit their accounts.

auger-hole: tiny place (an auger being a carpenter's piercer).

augure: augury.

authorized by: attributed to.

avouch: vouch for.

bade (pronounced 'bad'): asked; told.

badged: marked.

bane: destruction.

barefaced: undisguised; open.

battle (noun): (i: 1.1.4:) battle;
(ii: 5.6.4:) division of an army.
bear: (i: 1.7.17:) exert;
(ii: 3.6.3, 17:) carry out;
bear in hand: deceive.
behind: 1.3.118: to come.
beldam: hag.
bellman: night-watchman.
Bellona: Roman war-goddess;
Bellona's bridegroom:
Macbeth as supreme warrior.
benison: blessing.
bent: resolved.
bestow: lodge.
bestride: protectively stand over.
betimes: (i: 3.4.134:) early;
(ii: 4.3.162:) quickly.
bill: list.
birthdom: fatherland.
blaspheme his breed: slander
his lineage.
blood-boltered: blood-plastered.
bodement: augury; presage.
bond (n.): (i: 3.2.54:) lease of
life; (ii: 4.1.84:) legal agreement
to fulfil a contract.
borne in hand: deceived.
botch (n.): flaw entailed by
clumsy work.
break (vb.): 1.7.48: declare; reveal.
breeched: covered;
unmannerly breeched:
indecently clad.
brinded: brindled: tabby.
broad: (i: 1.6.17:) extensive;
(ii: 3.4.23:) unrestrained;
(iii: 3.6.21:) bold; frank.
broil: confused fighting.
bruit (vb.): proclaim.
buy: 1.7.32: gain; win.
called: 1.3.40: said to be.
card: compass-card.
careless trifle: carefree triviality.
casing (adj.): surrounding.

cast (vb.): 2.3.37: (a) throw
down; (b) vomit; **cast the
water**: analyse the urine.
catch: 1.5.17: seize.
cause (n.): (i: 3.1.33:) matter;
(ii: 3.4.137:) consideration;
(iii: 5.2.3:) basis of accusation;
(iv: 5.2.15:) medical case;
sickness.
censure: judgement.
chalice: 1.7.11: (a) goblet;
(b) wine-cup used in the Mass.
challenge (vb.): blame; accuse.
chamberlain: bedroom-attendant.
champion: 3.1.71: (a) oppose;
(b, less likely) support.
charge (n.): (i: 2.2.6:) office;
duty; (ii: 4.3.20:) command.
chaudron: chawdron: entrails.
check: rebuke.
choppy: chapped; cracked.
chops: jaws.
chough: jackdaw.
chuck: chick (affectionate term).
clear: innocent; spotless.
clearness: freedom from suspicion.
clept: called; named.
cling: 5.5.40: shrivel (*O.E.D.*).
close (vb.): (i: 3.1.98:) enclose;
(ii: 3.2.16:) heal; join.
close (adj.): secret; hidden.
closet: cabinet.
cloudy: 3.6.41: (a) angry;
(b) sullen.
coign of vantage: handy corner;
advantageous location.
colours: S.D. at 5.2, 5.4, etc.:
(a) ensigns; (b) standards;
(c) both.
combined: colluding.
combustion: civil uproar.
commend: 1.7.11: offer.
commission: **in commission**:
appointed to the task.

compassed: surrounded.

composition: armistice.

compt: **in compt**: already combined like a set of accounts.

confound: ruin; destroy.

confused: disorderly.

confusion: destruction.

conjure: formally invoke.

consent: 2.1.26: (a) complicity; (b) advice.

consequence: (i: 1.3.127; 1.7.3:) outcome; (ii: 5.3.5:) future event.

constancy: firmness; courage.

construction: 1.4.12: (a) nature; (b) intention.

continent: 4.3.64: (a) chaste; (b) restraining.

convey: secretly contrive.

convince: vanquish.

copy: 3.2.43: (a) pattern; image; (b) tenure.

corporal: (i: 1.3.82:) corporeal; (ii: 1.7.80:) bodily.

countenance (vb.): 2.3.77: (a) face; (b) fit; suit.

course (n.): (i: 2.2.39:) part of meal; (ii: 5.7.2:) onset of dogs in bear-baiting.

course (vb.): chase.

cousin: (a) cousin; (b) kinsman; (c) dear associate.

cowed: intimidated.

coz: 'cousin': dear associate.

crack: 1.2.37: explosive charge; **crack of Doom**: 4.1.117: (a) thunder-peal of Doomsday; (b) eruption of Doomsday.

crave: beg.

cribbed: held in small space, e.g. ox-stall.

crossed: impeded.

dainty: punctilious.

dareful: boldly.

dear: 5.2.3: (a) heartfelt; (b) honourable; (c) dire.

deer: 4.3.206: (a) deer; (b) dear ones.

degree: rank.

delicate: 1.6.10: (a) delightful; (b) delicious; (c) mild.

deliver: communicate.

demand: ask.

demi-wolf: 3.1.93: (a) cross between wolf and dog; (b) wolf-like dog.

deny: 3.4.129: refuse.

dignity: prestige.

direness: horror.

disbursèd: paid out.

discovery: reported reconnaissance.

disjoint: disintegrate.

disorder: 3.4.111: (a) agitation of mind; (b) commotion.

dispatch (n.): management.

dispatch (vb.): (i: 3.4.15:) slay; (ii: 5.3.50:) hasten.

displaced: banished.

dispute: resist.

distance: 3.1.115: discord (*O.E.D.*).

distempered: 5.2.15: (a) diseased; (b) disorderly.

division: 4.3.96: (a) variation; (b) descant.

doubt (n.): 3.4.25: anxiety.

doubt (vb.): 4.2.66: fear; **doubt it nothing**: are sure of it.

doubtful: fearful.

drab (n.): whore.

drenchèd: 1.7.68: (a) drowned; (b) sodden.

dudgeon: wooden hilt (*O.E.D.*).

dunnest: darkest.

duty: respect; reverence.

ecstasy: 3.2.25; 4.3.170: (a) torment; (b) madness.

effect: (i: 1.5.46:) fulfilment;
  (ii: 5.1.9:) manifestation.
egg: 4.2.82: senseless little
  offspring.
eminence: **Present him eminence**: Honour him above all.
encounter: welcome.
endure: (i: 5.4.9:) tolerate;
  (ii: 5.5.36:) suffer.
enkindle: incite.
epicure: sensual hedonist.
ere, or ere: before.
establish: bestow; settle.
estate: 1.4.37: (a) succession;
  (b) power and property;
  estate of the world: global
  order.
eterne: perpetual.
Evil: **'The Evil'**: scrofula.
except: 1.2.39: unless.
exeunt: they go out.
exit: he or she goes out.
expedition: rapid expression.
fact: crime.
faculties: powers.
fantastical: imaginary.
farrow: litter of pigs.
fatal: fateful; ominous.
favour: (i: 1.3.62; 1.3.150:)
  indulgence; (ii: 1.5.71: a) face,
  (b) appearance.
fee-grief: one person's private
  grief.
fell: cruel; **fell of hair**: head of
  hair.
fenny: 4.1.12: (a) muddy;
  (b) fenland.
field: battlefield.
file (n.): list; catalogue.
file (vb.): 3.1.64: defile.
fillet: slice.
finis (Latin): the end.
firstling: (i: 4.1.147: a: lit.:) first
  offspring; (b: fig.:) first idea;

(ii: 4.1.148: a: lit.:) first
  offspring; (b: fig.:) first action.
fit (n.): 3.4.21, 55: paroxysm of
  fever; **fits o'th'season**:
  disorders of the time.
fitful: subject to paroxysms.
flaw: gust of emotion.
flighty: swift; fleeting.
flung out: 2.4.16: (a) kicked
  out; (b) burst out.
flourish: fanfare at a ceremonial
  entry or exit.
flout: mock; insult.
foisons: abundance.
forbid: 1.3.22: (a) shunned;
  (b) accursed.
forced: reinforced.
forge (vb.): invent.
fork: forked tongue.
fountain: 2.3.19: source.
frailties: **naked frailties**: exposed
  weaknesses (e.g. tears of grief).
franchised: free; guiltless.
free (vb.): 3.6.35: banish.
free (adj.): (i: 3.6.36:) abundant;
  (ii: 5.9.21:) liberated.
free (adv.): 2.1.19: abundantly.
fret: (i: 4.1.91:) resist;
  (ii: 5.5.25:) agitate.
frieze: area between lintel and
  cornice.
fry: 4.2.83: (a) offspring; (b) spawn.
furbished: 1.2.32: (a) polished;
  (b) fresh.
fury: 2.3.103: (a) frenzy;
  (b) wild rage.
gallowglass: follower of an Irish
  or a Scottish chieftain.
general (adj.): (i: 3.4.23:) uncon-
  strained; (ii: 3.4.90; 4.3.196:)
  widespread.
Genius: guardian spirit.
gentle: (i: 1.6.3: a) noble;
  (b) mild; (c) made mild;

(ii: 3.4.77: a) made mild;
(b) civilised.

gently: quietly; unresistingly.

germen: seed.

get: 1.3.68: beget.

gibbet: 4.1.66: (a) post and cage
for suspending corpses;
(b) gallows.

gin: 4.2.35: trap.

'gins: begins.

give out: 4.3.192: show.

glass: 4.1.119: (a) mirror;
(b, perhaps) crystal ball.

go: 3.1.91: pass;
go off: 5.9.2: die.

golden: 1.7.33: glowing;
splendid; **golden round**:
crown.

Golgotha: 1.2.40: (a) place of
skulls; (b) burial-ground;
(c) charnel-house; (d) location
of the Crucifixion.

goose: 2.3.14: (a) tailor's
smoothing-iron; (b) the bird;
goose look: (a) white face;
(b) foolish face; (c) scared
look.

Gorgon: mythical snake-haired
female whose look petrified
men.

gospelled: taught by the Bible.

gout: clot; thick drop.

grace (n.): (i: 1.3.56; 2.3.91:)
honour; (ii: 4.3.23, 24, 159:)
holiness.

grace (vb.): 3.4.41, 45: honour.

graft: implant.

grandam: grandmother.

grave (adj.): weighty.

Gray-Malkin: Little Grey Mall
[or Moll] (name of grey cat).

gripe: grasp.

growing: 1.4.29: (a: lit.:) growth;
(b: fig.:) advancement.

guise: custom.

gulf: gullet.

half-world: global hemisphere.

happiness: good fortune.

harbinger: officer preceding a
monarch to procure lodgings.

harm: 3.5.7; 4.3.55: evil,
wickedness.

harness: armour.

harp: 4.1.74: (a) express;
(b) guess.

Harpier (name of a devil):
(perhaps) Harpy-like.

haunt: 1.6.9: usually reside.

hautboy: early form of oboe.

having: 1.3.57: possession.

heat-oppressèd: fevered.

Heaven: 4.3.6: (a) abode of
God; (b) the sky.

heavily: sorrowfully.

heavy: 2.1.7: (a) weighty;
(b) powerful; (c) soporific.

Heccat: Hecate: goddess of the
underworld and witchcraft.

hedge-pig: hedgehog.

hermit: 1.6.20: (a: lit.:)
beadsman; (b: fig.:) debtor.

hold: (i: 1.5.53:) stop;
(ii: 3.6.25:) withhold;
(iii: 4.2.19:) accept; believe.

home (adv.): 1.3.121: to the full.

homely: 4.2.66: (a) humble;
(b) plain.

honour: 3.4.40; 4.2.64: nobility.

hose: **French hose**: breeches,
variously baggy or tight.

housekeeper: watchdog.

howlet: owl or owlet.

hurly-burly: martial confusion.

husbandry: thrift.

Hyrcan: of Hyrcania (region
near Caspian Sea), noted for
tigers.

'ild: yield: reward.

illness: badness.
impress: (i: 4.1.95:) conscript;
(ii: 5.8.10:) imprint.
incarnadine: turn blood-red.
Inch (from Gaelic): Island;
Saint Colmè's Inch:
Inchcomb, St. Columba's
Island.
inform: manifest itself.
ingredience: contents.
inhabit: 3.4.106: (a) harbour;
(b) stay in.
initiate: novice's.
insane: insanity-inducing.
intelligence: information.
intemperance: excess.
interdiction: exclusion.
interest: **bosom interest**: deep
trust.
intrenchant: invulnerable.
inventor: contriver.
jealousies: suspicions.
juggling: cheating.
jump (vb.): 1.7.7: (a) leap over;
(b) dodge; (c) risk.
jutty: overhang.
kern: Scottish or Irish foot-
soldier.
knell is knolled: death-knell is
tolled.
lace (vb.): 2.3.109: diversify with
streaks of colour (*O.E.D.*).
lapped: wrapped.
large: 3.4.11: unrestrained.
largesse: rewards; bounty.
latch (vb.): catch.
lated: belated.
lave: wash.
lavish: wild; prodigal.
lay on: 5.8.33: strike hard.
lees: dregs.
lid: **penthouse lid**: (a: lit.:)
overhanging roof; (b: fig.:)
eye-lid.

liege: lord.
lily-livered: cowardly.
limbec: alembic: distilling
apparatus.
lime: glue to grip birds.
limited service: appointed duty.
line (vb.): reinforce.
list (n.): tournament-area.
lodged: (i: 2.2.25) in a room;
(ii: 4.1.55:) beaten down.
loon: fool.
luxurious: lecherous.
maggot-pie: magpie.
mansionry: home-building.
mark: (i: 1.2.28; 4.3.169; 5.1.35:)
note; (ii: 1.7.75:) stain.
marshal (vb.): usher.
martlet: 1.6.4: (a) swift;
(b) house-martin.
mated: baffled.
maw: 3.4.73; 4.1.23: craw:
gullet and first stomach.
measured: proportionate to.
med'cine: 5.2.27: healer.
memorize: 1.2.40: (a) bring to
mind; (b) make memorable.
mere: 4.3.89, 152: sheer, utter.
metaphysical: supernatural.
mettle: 1.7.73: (a) spirit;
strength of character;
(b) metal.
minion: darling; loved
favourite.
minister (n.): 1.5.47: attendant
spirit.
minutely: 5.2.18: every minute.
mischief: 1.5.49: (a) disturbance;
(b) evil-doing.
missive: messenger.
modern: ordinary; commonplace.
modest: moderating.
moe: more (in number).
more and less: 5.4.12: high and
low.

mortal: (i: 1.5.40; 3.4.82; 4.3.3:)
  lethal; (ii: 5.3.5: a) human;
  (b) lethal.
mortality: human life.
mortified: dead.
motive: incentive.
mould: bodily form.
mousing: 2.4.13: which usually
  preys on mice.
move (vb.): 3.4.48: trouble.
mummy: mummified flesh.
murther: murder.
muse (vb.): wonder.
napkin: 2.3.5: (a) hand-towel;
  (b) handkerchief.
nature: (i: 3.4.28:) life;
  (ii: 3.4.30:) vitality.
naught (n.): nothing.
naught (adj.): worthless.
nave: navel.
navigation: shipping.
near: 2.3.137: (a) close;
  (b) closer; **near'st of life:**
  3.1.117: (probably) heart.
nerve: 3.4.103: sinew (*O.E.D.*).
nice: detailed.
night-gown: dressing-gown.
nimbly: breezily.
noise: 4.1.106: musical sound.
nonpareil: paragon.
Norway: 1.2.51: Norway's King.
Norweyan: Norwegian.
note: note of expectation: list
  of expected guests; **of dreadful
  note:** 3.2.49: (a) of a dreadful
  nature; (b) to become
  notoriously dreadful.
notion: mind.
oblivious: oblivion-inducing.
offerings: ritual sacrifices.
office: (i: 2.1.14:) functionary;
  (ii: 3.3.3:) duty.
old: 2.3.2: ample.
omnes (Latin): all.

once: 5.5.15: ever.
out: 4.3.183: in armed revolt.
overcharged: additionally loaded.
overcome: overcast.
owe: 1.3.77; 1.4.10; 3.4.114: own.
pace: petty pace: 5.5.20:
  (a) trivial motion; (b) slow
  progress; (c) narrow passage.
paddock: toad.
pall (vb.): shroud.
palter: equivocate.
parted: departed: died.
passed in probation with:
  proved in detail to.
passion: outburst of emotion.
patch (n.): fool.
peak, and pine: waste away
  and decline.
pendant: 1.6.8: (a) suspended;
  (b) wedged-in.
penthouse: 1.3.21: (a: lit.:) overhanging roof; (b: fig.:) eyelid.
perfect: (i: 1.5.2:) reliable; (ii:
  3.1.107; 3.4.21:) completely
  sound; (iii: 4.2.64:) well
  versed; knowledgeable.
physic (vb.): 2.3.46: remedy.
pitfall: fowler's trap (concealed
  pit).
Pit of Acheron: entrance to Hades.
point: at a point: fully prepared.
portable: bearable.
posset: drink of hot milk and
  liquor.
post: rapid messenger.
posters: swift travellers.
power: 4.3.185; 5.2.1; 5.6.7:
  army.
practice: skill.
predominance (astrol.): superior
  influence.
present (adj.): immediate.
**pretence: undivulged
  pretence:** hidden purpose.

pretend: aspire to.

pride of place: highest point.

probation: passed in probation with: proved in detail to.

procreant: for offspring.

profess: (i: 4.1.50:) claim skill in; (ii: 5.7.28:) avows.

profound: 3.5.24: (a) dangling low; (b) potent.

proof: 1.2.54: (a) proven strength; (b) strong steel.

proper stuff: private rubbish.

proportion: full allocation.

prospect: range of vision.

prosperous: (i: 1.3.74:) thriving; (ii: 3.1.21:) profitable.

protest (vb.): proclaim.

provoke: stimulate.

purge (n.): 5.2.28: purifier.

purge (vb.): purify.

purveyor: arranger of food–supplies.

push (n.): 5.3.20: (a) thrust; attack; (b) endeavour.

quarry: (i: 1.2.14: a) quarrel; (b) object of pursuit; (ii: 4.3.206:) slaughter.

quell (n.): slaughter.

question (vb.): 2.3.125: discuss; analyse.

rancours: 3.1.66: (a: lit.:) bitterness; (b: fig.:) poison.

rapt: lost in reverie; preoccupied.

ravelled: tangled.

raven up: devour.

ravined: glutted.

receipt: receptacle, container.

receive: 1.7.74, 77: accept as true.

recoil: retreat; give way.

reflection: return.

relation: (i. 3.4.125:) connection; (ii: 4.3.173:) report.

relish: trace.

remembrancer: prompter.

remorse: 1.5.43: (a) pity; (b) relenting.

rendered: surrendered.

repeat upon: recite about.

repetition: report.

rest (vb.): 1.6.20: remain.

retreat: 5.9, S.D. : signal (e.g. trumpet-call) to recall troops.

ronyon: (perhaps) mangy creature.

roofed: under one roof.

round: (i: 1.5.27; 4.1.88:) crown; (ii: 4.1.130:) round dance.

rouse: rise.

rub (n.): 3.1.133: roughness.

rugged: (i: 3.2.27: a) furrowed; (b) frowning; (ii: 3.4.100:) rough.

rump-fed: 1.3.7: (a) fed on rump meat; (b) fat-buttocked.

Saint Colmè's Inch: Inchcomb (island in Firth of Forth).

saucy: insubordinate.

save: 1.2.47: preserve.

scanned: analysed.

scape: escape.

scarf up: blindfold.

school (vb.): control; regulate.

scorched: slashed.

score (n.): debt.

scour: clear; purge.

scruple: doubt.

season: 3.4.142: seasoning: preservative.

security: naïve confidence.

seeling: 3.2.51: (a: lit.:) sewing shut the eyelids (of a hawk); (b: fig.:) blinding

self: 3.4.143: private, personal; self abuse: 3.4.143: (a) personal aberration; (b) private affliction.

self-comparisons: matching qualities.

sennet: musical flourish or fanfare.

sense: 5.1.23: awareness.

sensible to: perceptible by.

sere: withered state.

sergeant: (then) commissioned officer, e.g. captain.

set: 3.1.112: bet.

settled: resolved.

sev'night: week.

shard-borne: 3.2.47: (a) borne on scaly wings; (b) born from dung.

shift away: slip away.

shough: shaggy dog.

sightless: invisible.

signs of nobleness: titles of honour.

Sinell: (chroniclers' version of) Finel, name of Macbeth's father.

single: (i: 1.3.141: a): integral; (b) weak; (ii: 1.6.16:) weak.

skipping: 1.2.30: (a) nimble; (b) absconding.

skirr: hasten to search.

slab (adj.): sludgy.

sleek (vb.): smooth.

sleeve: 2.2.37: (a) sleeve of garment; (b) sleave: filament of silk.

slivered: cut or torn off.

slope (vb.): drop.

smacking of: tainted by.

solely: absolutely.

solemn: formal.

sole name: name alone.

sooth: truth.

sore: (i: 2.2.38:) tiresome; (ii: 2.4.3:) dire.

sorry: 2.2.20, 21; 3.2.9: woeful, wretched.

sovereign: 5.2.30: (a) excellent; (b) remedial.

speculation: ability to see

spongy: soaked; drunken.

sprite: spirit; ghost.

stamp (n.): coin or medal.

stanchless: insatiable.

stand: 3.1.4: continue; **stand to't:** 3.3.15: (a) get ready; (b) be resolute; **stand upon:** insist on.

start (n.): 3.4.63: impulse.

start (vb.): (i: 4.1.116; 5.2.23:) jump; (ii: 5.5.15:) startle.

state: keeps her state: remains on her throne.

station: place.

staves: poles.

stay: 4.3.142: await; **stay upon:** wait for.

still: 3.1.21: constantly.

straight: very soon.

strange: (i: 1.3.145:) unfamiliar; (ii: 3.4.113:) a stranger.

studied: fully prepared.

suborned: bribed.

sudden: 4.3.59: (a) impetuous; (b) violent.

suggestion: temptation.

sundry: various.

surcease: 1.7.4: (a) death; (b) murder.

sway: 5.3.9: govern my actions.

sweltered: sweated.

swoop: 4.3.219: (a) pounce; (b) total victory.

take off: 3.1.104; 5.9.37: destroy.

taking-off: 1.7.20: murder.

Tarquin: Roman King who raped Lucrece.

teem: give birth to.

temper (n.): character.

Thane: 1.2.45: (a) Baron; (b) Chief (of a clan).

thought: upon a thought: in an instant.

thrall: captive.

time: 1.5.62-3; 1.7.81; 4.3.72: present society.

title: 4.3.34: (a) claim to throne;
(b) name (here 'tyranny');
titles: 4.2.7: possessions.

top (vb.): surpass.

tower (vb.): soar up.

trace (vb.): follow.

train (n.): 4.3.118: (a) lure;
(b) trick.

trammel up: enmesh; ensnare.

transpose: change.

treatise: story.

trenchèd: deep

trifled: made trivial.

tugged with: mauled by (O.E.D.).

unbend: relax.

undeeded: unused.

undone: ruined.

unfix: loosen; dishevel.

unmake: 1.7.54: (a) demoralise;
(b) ruin.

unmannerly: disgracefully.

unrough: unbearded.

unseamed: ripped open.

unsex me: remove my womanly
nature.

untitled: without legal claim to
rule

uproar (vb.): utterly disrupt.

use (n.): **against the use of
nature**: unnaturally.

using: 3.2.12: becoming used to.

utterance: lethal uttermost.

valued file: 3.1.94: (a) valuable
analysis; (b) evaluative
categorisation.

vantage: 1.3.114: advantage; **coign
of vantage**: convenient corner;
surveying vantage: seeing an
advantageous opportunity.

vault (n.): wine-cellar.

virtue: 4.3.156: good power.

visited: afflicted.

visitings: feelings.

vizard: mask.

wake: 3.6.31: arouse.

want: 3.6.8: lack.

wanton: unrestrained.

warrant (n.): justification.

warranted: justified.

wassail: carousal.

wasteful: devastating.

watch (vb.): (i: 5.1.1:) keep
watch at night; (ii: 5.1.9:)
remain awake.

watcher: one who stays awake
at night.

water-rug: (perhaps) shaggy
water-dog (O.E.D.).

weal: 3.4.77; 5.2.27: society;
nation.

weighed: (i: 1.3.155:) assessed;
(ii: 4.3.90:) balanced.

well: 5.2.6: probably.

Weyard, Weyward: 1.3.33;
1.5.7; 2.1.21; 3.1.2; 3.4.134;
4.1.136: (a) Wayward; perverse; (b) Strange; unnatural;
(c) 'Weird', i.e. fateful.

while: 3.1.43: until.

win: 1.3.124, 126: win over.

wink at: not see.

withal: (i: 1.5.29; 2.1.16:) with;
(ii: 4.3.41:) also.

within: 1.2, S.D.; 1.3.30, S.D.,
etc.: off-stage.

worm: young snake.

wrack: ruin; **wracked**: wrecked.

wrought: (i: 1.3.150:) agitated;
(ii: 2.1.20; 3.1.81:) acted;
(iii: 3.5.22:) completed.

yesty: yeasty: frothy.

younker: young man.